MILITARY POWER

CAN DETERRENCE LAST?

MILITARY POWER

A series produced in conjunction with
The Royal United Services Institute for Defence Studies

GENERAL EDITOR   GROUP CAPTAIN DAVID BOLTON,
RAF (Ret)
EDITOR   JENNIFER SHAW, MA, BSc(Econ)

In the highly dangerous world in which we live, the subject of defence, and of all kinds of warfare, becomes increasingly relevant in day-to-day life. These studies – concise, topical, well written, meticulously balanced, and reasonably priced – not only provide the reader with background information, but also offer a platform for differing but expert views. Each book carries an introduction by an eminent figure, and is aimed at the general reader as well as at those with a professional interest.

MILITARY POWER

CAN DETERRENCE LAST?
Peace Through a Nuclear Strategy

TIMOTHY GARDEN

Foreword by Correlli Barnett

**THE ROYAL UNITED SERVICES
INSTITUTE FOR DEFENCE STUDIES**

BUCHAN & ENRIGHT, PUBLISHERS,
LONDON

First published in 1984 by
Buchan & Enright, Publishers, Limited
53 Fleet Street, London EC4Y 1BE

British Library Cataloguing in Publication Data

Garden, Timothy
Can deterrence last?—(Military power)
1. Deterrence (Strategy)   2. Atomic warfare
I. Title   II. Series
355′.0217   U162.6

ISBN 0-907675-32-8

Photoset in North Wales by
Derek Doyle & Associates, Mold, Clwyd
Printed in Great Britain at
The Pitman Press, Bath

CONTENTS

ABBREVIATIONS

ABM	ANTI-BALLISTIC MISSILE
CBM	CONFIDENCE BUILDING MEASURE
CEA	COMMISSARIAT À L'ENERGIE ATOMIQUE
CSCE	CONFERENCE ON SECURITY AND COOPERATION IN EUROPE
CTB	COMPREHENSIVE TEST BAN
ICBM	INTERCONTINENTAL BALLISTIC MISSILE
KT	KILOTON
MBFR	MUTUAL AND BALANCED FORCE REDUCTIONS
MIRV	MULTIPLE INDEPENDENTLY-TARGETABLE RE-ENTRY VEHICLE
MT	MEGATON
NATO	NORTH ATLANTIC TREATY ORGANISATION
NPT	NON-PROLIFERATION TREATY
PAL	PERMISSIVE ACTION LINK
PNE	PEACEFUL NUCLEAR EXPLOSION
R and D	RESEARCH AND DEVELOPMENT
SALT	STRATEGIC ARMS LIMITATION TALKS
SIOP	SINGLE INTEGRATED OPERATIONAL PLAN
SIPRI	STOCKHOLM INTERNATIONAL PEACE RESEARCH INSTITUTE
SSBN	NUCLEAR-POWERED BALLISTIC MISSILE SUB-MARINE
US	UNITED STATES
USSR	UNION OF SOVIET SOCIALIST REPUBLICS

FOR
Sue, Alexandra and Antonia

PREFACE

BY GROUP CAPTAIN DAVID BOLTON
DIRECTOR RUSI

Founded in 1831 with the Duke of Wellington as its first president, the Royal United Services Institute for Defence Studies has operated since 1860 under Royal Charter charged with examining the full range of questions related to the military sciences. The RUSI is a fully independent body but its membership largely comprises those with authority and responsibility, coupled with practical good sense, within their own particular field. In addition to being the professional Institute of the Armed Forces, the RUSI's membership includes those from industry and academe, the media, civil servants and parliamentarians, as well as the military. The Institute therefore acts as a bridge between different constituencies and disciplines concerned with defence by drawing on the diverse interests and responsibilities of its members. The RUSI further seeks to enhance informed opinion and to encourage a wider understanding and debate of important defence issues. In this, the Military Power Series is designed to play an important part by questioning and helping to formulate ideas on topical subjects of the moment.

'Can Deterrence Last?' is such a topic and Timothy Garden has been associated with the practical aspects of deterrence for most of his RAF service. As deterrence is largely a matter of perception it is of fundamental importance that the view-points of the nuclear powers, as well as those with a potential nuclear capability, are examined. If deterrence is to work then its basic theory needs to be understood and the prospects for future stability in the areas of technological advance, arms control agreements, as well as military strategies, all need to be explored. These matters are directly addressed by Timothy Garden in this first book in the Military Power Series which marks a new and professional association between the RUSI and Buchan & Enright. Defence questions and, in particular, nuclear issues, give rise to strong emotion. Rational argument provides a better response and a firmer basis of knowledge. It is the perception of realities, as opposed to popular myth and emotion, which has also long prompted the work of the RUSI and it is similarly consonant with the aims of this Military Power Series.

In any democratic society, public understanding and support are fundamental to sustaining a viable policy for the security of essential freedoms and interests. It is hoped that an objective perspective will be provided in this book and its successors to further public interest and awareness.

FOREWORD

CORRELLI BARNETT

In 1914 and again in 1939, it was possible for the great military powers to consider war in classic Clausewitzian terms as an instrument of policy; one among other such instruments like diplomacy or economic pressure for achieving national objectives in the competitive arena of power relations. In 1914, all the major belligerents imagined that the killing and destruction would take place on enemy territory as their armies carried out war-winning offensives, while in the meantime their own homelands, their seats of political and industrial power, remained unscathed. Only in the course of four years of slow-burning attrition was this confident sense of immunity from the direct scourge of war gradually eroded. Even in 1939, with the example of the cumulative destructiveness of the Great War before them, it was possible for the Nazi leadership to march against Poland in the belief that it had to face no more than a local campaign against a feebler power, and that no inevitable or devastating consequence could befall Germany itself. Again it took long years of war before such retribution reached the point of destroying Germany as a modern industrial society.

But with the coming of the nuclear age, above all the thermo-nuclear age, it is no longer possible for any great military power to consider war against another as a rational, usable, instrument of policy; no longer possible for general staffs and cabinets in an international crisis to take decisions that risk, or bring nearer, the outbreak of armed conflict in that spirit of levity, certainly irresponsibility, in which Austria-Hungary in July 1914 issued its ultimatum to Serbia, or Nazi Germany fomented the Polish crisis in August-September 1939. For there can be no illusion now that the destruction will only occur far off in another country. It is as if in 1914 the consequences of Austria's going to war with Serbia were known in advance by the Austrians to be the immediate and inevitable destruction of Vienna and much else besides; as if in 1939 the consequences of Germany invading Poland were known to be the instant production of those scenes in Berlin, Hamburg, Dresden and the Ruhr that in fact took six years to complete.

Thus there can be no successful 'Schlieffen Plan' or 'Blitzkrieg' with nuclear weapons against another nuclear power. Nuclear weapons cannot serve as Clausewitzian instruments of national policy in the rivalry between nuclear great powers. They can only dissuade, by their menacing presence in the cupboard, the use of nuclear weapons by a hostile power, or prevent the employment of nuclear blackmail in diplomacy. Their only rational utility is therefore as a stand-off, as 'deterrence'.

It is not only that nuclear war itself is unthinkable as a profitable instrument of policy, it is also that it renders even conventional conflict between nuclear powers so loaded with the risk of ultimate nuclear devastation that such conventional conflict too has been rendered obsolete as an instrument of policy in great power rivalry.

Given that thermonuclear armouries are unprofitable, indeed suicidally unusable, as the means of settling quarrels between nuclear states, there remains only the complex question of 'deterrence' itself. This, coupled with awareness of the appalling potential destructive power of those armouries, has kept academics, military men, politicians and disarmers busy since the 1950s debating on paper and platforms and in committees. The topic of nuclear deterrence has come to supply something of the intellectual role of religion in the Middle Ages, in that it has inspired a new generation of nuclear 'theologians' or schoolmen, mostly in American think-tanks, to argue the subtleties of deterrent and conflict theory with the ingenuity of a St Thomas Aquinas; and equally inspired a new breed of itinerant preachers blazing with fervour, warning of the wrath to come, and calling on men to nuclear repentance.

The problem for the non-specialist who would understand 'deterrence' and inform himself of the differing views about the nature of effective deterrence adopted by the various nuclear powers (and hence their actual nuclear policies) has lain in trying to find a short, lucid, dispassionate and yet authoritative reference book. It is this hitherto empty slot that Group Captain Garden's *Can Deterrence Last?* so excellently fills.

The book is the fruit of a year at Cambridge University working for the degree of M Phil in International Relations, when Group Captain Garden was able to sieve through the massive literature of deterrent theory and at the same time study the evolution of differing national policies towards nuclear weapons. He brings to his analysis an extra dimension of understanding, in that he is a serving airman who has himself lived with the responsibility of commanding a squadron of V-bombers with nuclear capability. He therefore knows at first hand the realities of what he is here writing about. His approach is practical and responsible as well as doubly well-informed. Moreover, the objectiveness of his analysis is enhanced by a studied coolness of language, and language mercifully free from unnecessary jargon.

Can Deterrence Last? opens with a clear and sceptical summary of the elements of deterrence theory as advanced by leading nuclear thinkers, discussing the role of such factors as a credible operational capability on the one hand and on the other a credible political will to respond with nuclear weapons if any enemy resorts to them. There follow succinct dossiers on the *raisons d'être* for, and historical development of, the nuclear deterrent systems of the US, Soviet Russia, Britain, France and China, with glances at potential if not actual nuclear powers like Israel and India. Group Captain Garden's book concludes with an examination of the political and technological factors that make for nuclear stability between the powers, hence reducing to the minimum the risk of a catastrophic nuclear exchange, or that make for a perilous instability. He perceives little hope for successful arms agreement, but believes that the best chance of continued stability lies in nuclear weapons systems that are invulnerable to a pre-emptive strike, so that an aggressor could never be sure of escaping retribution. He regards better 'hot-line' communication links, coupled with the mutual sparing of national leadership centres in order to ensure command and control in the event of an 'accidental' nuclear discharge, as further means of enhancing stability. Group Captain Garden cannot offer some magical escape route from the fact of the existence of nuclear weapons, but he does leave us with the hopeful prognosis that it is this very existence which alone can best guard against their use.

Can Deterrence Last? ought to be in the library of every educational institution and on the bookshelf of every concerned person, for it constitutes an essential text for anyone wishing to form, or express, an opinion about nuclear weapons and their role in international relationships.

CORRELLI BARNETT
1984

AUTHOR'S INTRODUCTION

The day when two army corps can annihilate one another in one second, all civilised nations, it is to be hoped, will recoil from war and discharge their troops.

ALFRED NOBEL in 1892[1]

The scale of destruction possible with nuclear weapons must exceed the wildest speculations of Alfred Nobel, yet his hopes for the resulting disarmament have not been fulfilled. Theories for the effects of nuclear weapons on international relations have blossomed in the past 38 years; and central to much of this 'deterrent theory' is the horror which Nobel foresaw, when he was inaugurating the prize for peace, and wished that he could 'invent a machine of such frightful efficiency for wholesale destruction that wars should thereby become altogether impossible'.[2]

Deterrence theories have tried to do many things: to explain the rationale for a current national posture; to predict the actions and responses of states in peace, in crises, and in war; to suggest strategies for the furtherance of foreign policy objectives; and to suggest equipment procurement to improve force effectiveness, world stability or national survivability. The major weakness of deterrence theory is its lack of supporting experimental evidence. While much may, and has been, inferred from international events which involve nuclear weapon states, the evidence is rarely conclusive. Since 1945, the key issue of when nuclear weapons would be used in anger has, fortunately, never been put to the conclusive test. The nuclear strategists in this period have developed intricate theories against a backcloth of rapid but largely untested technological innovation. Their ideas are important, not solely because of their validity or otherwise, but also because of the influence that they may have had on the shaping of national strategies. That world peace may depend on a capability to exterminate, virtually instantaneously, a significant portion of mankind is bizarre; yet the possible results of a nuclear conflict make the need for maintaining peace, a matter of prime importance.

The first part of this book looks at the theoretical concepts of nuclear deterrence, and draws out the various schools of thought which have emerged in the short period of the nuclear age. That some theories contradict others, or result in quite opposite conclusions, is not surprising given the inevitable subjectivity of any analysis which depends on predicting human reactions to given circumstances. Having examined the theory, the practice in each of the nuclear weapon states is studied in the second part. We look at how and why nuclear weapons were obtained by each state, and the rationale for their possession today and for the future. Finally, having put the theory in the context, those factors which bear upon the stability of the system are considered.

The stability of the system must be the key area of concern for strategists and decision-makers alike. It is no part of my intention to provide Utopian solutions to the world's problems. The aim of this book is to highlight those areas which have an influence on future stability, are amenable to change, and for which there are incentives to implement the necessary changes. Through such examination, not only will the question of whether deterrence can last be answered, but options for improving its robustness will be offered.

As a serving officer in the Royal Air Force, I have had ample opportunity to think about the practicality of nuclear deterrence, particularly while flying Canberras in Germany and commanding a Vulcan strategic bomber squadron. The research for this book is drawn from a year spent at Magdalene College, Cambridge, working for an MPhil degree in International Relations. The help of Dr Philip Towle, at the University, was invaluable in bringing together my thoughts in this volume. Those thoughts, however, do remain entirely my own and do not necessarily reflect official opinion.

TIMOTHY GARDEN
Bracknell 1984

Part I

Nuclear Deterrence Theory

CHAPTER ONE

THE THINKING MAN'S BOMB

Thus far the chief purpose of our military establishment has been to win wars. From now on its chief purpose must be to avert them. It can have almost no other useful purpose.

BERNARD BRODIE in 1946[1]

The destruction of Hiroshima and Nagasaki in 1945 demonstrated to the world the unprecedented scale of devastation which could now be achieved from a single attack. The death and disruption which had needed vast numbers of aircraft, over a number of hours, using conventional high explosive bombs, could now be obtained with a single weapon in an instant. Even this power was soon to be dwarfed by the theoretically limitless energy of the thermonuclear bomb. The American strategist, Bernard Brodie, appreciated the significance of this development from the earliest days of the atomic age. He could visualise no effective defence against such weapons and so nuclear deterrence could be the only practical future strategy.

The decision to go to war is an act of choice by a state. The choice may be made for offensive purposes, in order to gain some advantage; or it may be for defensive reasons, in order to protect some vital interest from an aggressor. In either event, the decision to go to war has been based on an assessment, which is not necessarily correct, that there is more to be gained, or less to be lost, by going to war rather than refraining from war. The essence of deterrence is the ability to convince a state, which has it in mind to go to war with you, that no such advantageous profit and loss assessment is possible. To achieve this happy position, a number of conditions must be met:

i Capability. *The deterring state must have the capability to ensure that the potential enemy will profit less by going to war than by refraining from war.*
ii Will. *The deterring state must have the will to use its capability if necessary.*
iii Credibility. *The potential enemy must know of, and believe in, both (i) and (ii).*
iv Rationality. *Each side must be sufficiently rational to base its conduct on an understanding of (i) to (iii).*

By examining each of these four conditions in detail, the various threads and paradoxes of deterrent theory emerge.

THE CAPABILITY TO DETER

What capability is necessary to ensure that no potential enemy can make the wrong deduction about his inevitable losses, should he go to war? Many had expected that the conventional strategic bombing, which was to come in World War II, would cause unacceptable devastation. In the event, the damage was not a decisive factor and the capability was not a deterrent. Brodie maintained that nuclear weapons are different because of the lack of warning time, the instantaneous destruction, the uselessness of shelters and the additional casualties from the delayed effects.[2] The United States Senate Committee on Foreign Relations commissioned a report, which was published in 1980, into the effects of a nuclear war. The report examines, as objectively as possible, the various outcomes of a range of conflicts in which nuclear weapons are used. The stark summary of the effects on either of the superpowers of a large scale attack shows the quite different deterrent capability of nuclear weapons from high explosive:

Summary of Effects
Case 4: Attack on range of military and economic targets using large fraction of existing arsenal.

Main causes of civilian damage: Blast and fallout; subsequent economic disruption; possible lack of resources to support surviving population or economic recovery. Possible breakdown of social order. Possible incapacitating psychological trauma.

Immediate Deaths: 20,000,000 – 160,000,000

Middle-term effects: Enormous economic destruction and disruption. If immediate deaths are in the low range, more tens of millions may die subsequently because the economy is unable to support them. Major question whether economic viability can be restored – key variables may be those of political and economic organisation. Unpredictable psychological effects.

Long-term effects: Cancer deaths and genetic damage in the millions; relatively insignificant in the attacked areas, but quite significant elsewhere in the world. Possibility of ecological damage.[3]

This summary describes what amounts to the destruction of the state. Indeed, elsewhere it explores the economic problems following an attack and points to the possibility that 'the future of civilization in the nations attacked would be in doubt'.[4] Other research has suggested that the use of between 500 and 2000 nuclear warheads could trigger a climatic catastrophe, which would carry with it the risk of the extinction of the human race.[5] In the early days of deterrence theory, attempts were made to quantify levels of assured destruction necessary to deter; modern nuclear arsenals leave little room for doubt that these levels have been achieved.

Nuclear weapons can therefore provide a level of destruction which, by any criteria, will leave a state worse off if it suffers a nuclear attack than if it takes a course of action which will not result in such an attack. One such course is to be deterred, the other is to prevent the nuclear attack from happening by destroying the opponent's capability. Thus to preserve a deterrent capability, a state must be able to deliver its weapons under all possible circumstances. Much concern has been expressed by the theorists over the possibility of preventative or pre-emptive attacks in which the deterring state is deprived of its retaliatory capability. A threatened state could reduce its risk of unacceptable damage by making the first strike against the other state's nuclear forces: a counter-force strike. As the French strategist, General Beaufre, said:

> *The conclusion was therefore that capacity for riposte was the key to nuclear deterrence, whereas capability to reduce the riposte was the key to nuclear initiative.*[6]

What is necessary is the ability to absorb a first strike, and yet still retain the capability to return a sufficiently devastating attack against all that the enemy values: a counter-value strike.

There is general agreement that the invulnerable second strike capability against the counter-value targets (which in practice would be cities) underpins any deterrent posture.

THE POLITICAL WILL

If the political will to use the nuclear weapon capability does not exist, then deterrence can only be achieved through bluff. As Herman Kahn explained:

> *If we are only pretending that we would do it, the credibility and therefore the deterrent value of our force is almost certain to be lessened by the automatic and inevitable leaks.*[7]

The question of credibility will be discussed later, but the factors which affect the real determination to use nuclear weapons *in extremis* are now considered.

Deterrence of a non-nuclear state by a nuclear weapon state ought to be straightforward. There should be no doubt that the nuclear state can devastate its non-nuclear opponent, while remaining unscathed itself. It is by no means clear, however, that any nuclear state, with the possible exception of Israel, has the will to use its nuclear weapons against a non-nuclear enemy. Leaving aside the examples of Hiroshima and Nagasaki, each time that the opportunity to use nuclear weapons has arisen, the nuclear state has limited itself to the use of conventional weapons only; even at the price of accepting limited defeat. It appears that the political will is lacking for practical, political and ethical reasons.

Brodie suggested a number of different reasons why nuclear weapons were not used in the Korean War.[8] The limited American stockpile was kept in reserve for Europe; the weapons were considered inappropriate for tactical targets; there was political pressure from the United Nations allies; the Soviets might use their bomb; there were distasteful racial implications in using atomic weapons first against the Japanese, and then against the Koreans and Chinese. Thomas Schelling, in 1960, highlighted the importance of a tradition of the non-use of nuclear weapons.[9] By making a 'tacit bargain' through the continued non-use, then the expectation grows that all crises will be solved without recourse to nuclear weapons, and stability is enhanced. Whether this restraint has been the conscious establishing of a tradition, moral repugnance or fear of other superpower involvement, the taboo has grown. It appears unlikely, unless the survival of a country was at stake – as could be the case in Israel – that nuclear weapons will be used against an enemy armed only with conventional weapons.

The political will to use nuclear weapons against another nuclear-armed state raises many of the fundamental questions of nuclear deterrence. Once each of two opposing states has invulnerable retaliatory forces, deterrence is mutual. The question then is whether, given the retaliatory power of the opponent, a state would ever have the will to use its weapons. Herman Kahn explored the consequences of a nuclear exchange in the 1960s, and considered that measures could be taken to limit the damage expected sufficiently to reinforce the will to use nuclear weapons. His view that civil defence measures, air defence improvements and targeting the enemy's nuclear weapons on the ground could so limit damage that the 'survivors will not envy the dead'[10] has lost credibility in the light of the growth of nuclear capabilities. Henry Kissinger, writing three years earlier, could not conceive of a meaningful victory in a total war, but he was concerned with the effect that this nuclear stalemate would have on his nation's strategy and diplomacy:

The costs of an all-out war are too fearful for it to be our only response to a challenge. Even if it could be won, we should seek to achieve our objectives at smaller sacrifice. Strategy can assist policy only by developing a maximum number of stages between total peace (which may mean surrender) and total war. It can increase the willingness of policy-makers to run risks only if it can demonstrate other means of preventing amputations than the threat of suicide.[11]

There is a widespread assumption that a government would have the will to use its nuclear capability in response to an all-out attack on the homeland. The rationality of this action will be considered later. This spasm response is the basis of mutual assured destruction deterrence. The worry that Kissinger was expressing was the need for appropriate responses to threats at levels beneath that of the destruction of the homeland. The extending of deterrence to cover a range of conflicts, including the defence of allies, is a recurring problem in the writings of strategists. If deterrence works, then a country will be self-deterred if it has no alternative but all-out war in any conflict. What is required is a range of options which will give the politician the chance to combat aggression with the appropriate level of defence. A conventional attack is met with a conventional defence; tactical nuclear weapons meet a nuclear response; limited strategic options of, for example, the destruction of one city, are returned in kind. The political will to use a capability to reply in kind is more likely to exist than the political will to cause a total war for limited objectives.

The range of options can be described as a 'flexible response' doctrine or a 'nuclear war-fighting' capability, depending on the view of the writer as to the motives of that state. In either case, it has a number of attractions to the political, military, scientific and strategic establishment. It gives the politician a wide range of options; it allows the military to equip and plan for a wide range of contingencies; it gives the scientist scope to develop new weapons; and the strategist can devise scenarios to justify the range of options. However, if every level of engagement is to be catered for, the potential cost can become very great. In admitting that military resources must be finite, the politician must admit also that the appropriate response available for any given level of aggression may be inadequate. The option then is to concede or to escalate. A conventional attack would be met with a conventional response, to the limits of the defending forces. If the defences do not hold, then battlefield nuclear weapons would be used to prevent defeat. This type of escalation scenario envisages a graduated increase in the level and extent of the battle until one side stops, having realised that it cannot win. In a symmetrical conflict between nuclear powers, it is difficult to see how the escalation of violence by one side can do anything except raise the level of the response. With the exception of the important tradition of the distinction between conventional and nuclear weapons, there is no natural stopping place on the slope to all-out war. Even if such firebreaks could be tacitly agreed, one study by Desmond Ball[12] gives little prospect for the practicalities of control of a war, once the nuclear threshold has been crossed.

If the practicalities of a particular flexible strategy are such that there is a strong possibility of any response to aggression leading to a strategic nuclear exchange, then the problem of the political will has not been solved. This difficulty is particularly acute in NATO strategy. Any use of nuclear weapons in Europe, at whatever level, is likely to result in massive devastation to the country which is the scene of the conflict. The political will might well exist in the United States to use battlefield nuclear weapons to stem a possible conventional defeat on European soil, if there were a strong belief that further escalation would not occur. In Europe, the attractions of limiting the destruction to the continent itself might be less strong. Indeed, there would be a desire to shelter under the greater deterrent threat of the American strategic guarantee. This would increase the pressure for rapid escalation if the nuclear threshold were crossed. The problems of the deterrent posture for Western Europe have given rise to two schools of thought. There are those who follow General Beaufre,[13] Henry Kissinger[14] and Glenn Snyder,[15] and maintain that the tactical nuclear weapons provide the essential graduated link between the strategic nuclear forces and the conventional forces. The expectation that the political will exists to meet aggression at the conventional level, but is likely to escalate to the strategic level, couples the strategic deterrent to all the other possible response levels. Those of the other school – Richard Garwin,[16] Lord Carver[17] and Fred Iklé,[18] for example – argue that the strategic deterrent is effective. A strong conventional force is usable, whereas the prospect of a nuclear battlefield in Europe would sap the political will of West European leaders.

While there is some force to both proposals, it is unlikely that either would make a great deal of difference in practice to the kind of decision which politicians would have to make in a crisis. While two of the European NATO powers – Britain and France – have their own deterrent forces, it would seem likely that at least one nuclear power would be prepared to honour its guarantees, and this aspect is discussed further when credibility is considered. The argument that conventional forces need to be increased to raise the nuclear threshold, and thus enhance deterrence, is valid only if it dissuades the opposition from adventurism. Conventional forces as a deterrent have had little success in the past, and if an increase in them signifies a reluctance to use nuclear weapons, then this may reduce the overall deterrent effect.

If the stark alternatives of suicide or surrender sap the political will, and the graduated devastation of the countries where the battle is fought is also politically controversial, the third strategy to consider is that of limited strategic options. In this case, the response to an act of aggression would be to carry out, either with or without warning, limited strategic strikes. The strikes could be on selected military, industrial or urban targets. If the action, plus the threat of further strikes, is sufficient to cause the adversary to withdraw, then this is a powerful form of deterrence. Escalation is, of course, still possible and indeed could be more likely following even a single strike on an enemy city, but it can be argued that the war would be more easily controlled than the fast moving events of the nuclear battlefield. One investigation in 1962 into the political will to carry through such a policy of limited strategic war concluded that it did not seem to offer a viable alternative to the normal counter-force strategy which existed.[19] However, since then, the technical capability to carry out accurate strategic attacks has improved considerably with the advent of better navigation systems, rapid retargeting facilities and a wide range of warhead yields. It is also entirely likely that the leaders of any nuclear countries would wish in a crisis to keep close personal control over the use of nuclear weapons, at least in the early stages. This would mean that the effective strategy might well become one of threats for very limited strikes, with deadlines set, followed by careful execution of the threat. Limited strategic options appear to be the more likely way nuclear weapons would be used, whatever the declared strategy or the force structure. In this case, there is some merit in questioning the usefulness of a tactical nuclear capability if it has an adverse effect on non-nuclear capability.

In summary, the political will to use the nuclear capability remains an uncertain area. The political will may be there for a spasm retaliation to an attack on the homeland. At lesser levels, the political will is questionable, whatever the force structure, given the expectation of escalation. In the event of a crisis and the failure of deterrence, the capability to threaten limited strategic strikes may serve to offer sufficient prospect of control to reinforce the political will.

CREDIBILITY

The credibility of a particular deterrent posture cannot be assigned some absolute value. It is a measure of the probability, as perceived by the potential enemy, that the deterring state has both the will and the capability to carry out an action which will make the planned aggression not worth doing. It is interesting to note that there is an interaction between the perception of capability and of will. For example, it is entirely credible that a conventionally armed invasion force would, normally, be met with a conventional defence: the political will is credible. However, the deterrent effect of this conventional defence posture is reduced if its capability to stop the invasion is perceived by the invader as low: the capability is not credible. At the other extreme, to threaten massive nuclear retaliation in response to a minor incursion may lack credibility, not through any doubt of the capability to make such an incursion less than worthwhile, but because of a disbelief in the political will to carry through such a policy. Where two states have an assured retaliation capability, it will seem especially unlikely that the defender will risk retribution by taking such heavy handed action against a small aggression. In general, the harsher the nuclear response, the more improbable that it will be employed, for fear that it will draw similar or worse retaliation.

In an attempt to rationalise the mutual perceptions of probabilities of action, some strategists have reduced the relationships between states to mathematical models. While no precision is claimed for the values attributed to specific probabilities, and to the profit and loss values of different outcomes, their authors claim that 'to express it in mathematical terms can provide a useful check on intuitive judgement.'[20] The methodology of game theory could be of value, when examining past crises, as a way of pointing to factors which merit detailed analysis. It is of limited application when dealing with the complexities of the decision-making processes, to produce answers to future problems which are as yet ill-defined. The Cuban missile crisis was a rare occasion on which there was some evidence of the perceived probabilities involved, and where the deductions from game theory give rather unconvincing results:

> *President Kennedy said that he thought the chances of war during the Cuban missile crisis were at least one in three. If he believed this, he either placed an incredibly high value on prevailing, or else he did not understand probability-utility calculus. It is hard to accept the notion that Kennedy thought the costs of war combined with twice the gains that would accrue if he won (the payoff for standing firm when the odds were two to one that the Russians would back down) were anything like equal to the value of losing combined with twice the value of a compromise (the payoff for backing down with the odds as stated).*[21]

As both ignorance and the conscious ignoring of probability-utility calculus are likely to be continuing features of crisis management, game theory offers little help in formulating deterrent strategy for the wide range of possible future scenarios. We shall not consider it further, but return to the subjective approach.

To make a deterrent threat credible, the deterrent state must signal its potential enemy that there is a significant probability that the appropriate retribution will be forthcoming. As we have seen, a convincing readiness to fight a nuclear war at any level can improve credibility. Measures such as civil defence, air defence and the complete integration of nuclear arms into battle plans make this posture more credible. As Kahn[22] pointed out, the deterrent posture would become completely credible if it could be made to be a totally automatic form of retaliation. Moves towards this can be made by adopting 'launch on warning' techniques and delegating nuclear release authority to the lowest levels. While these measures may improve credibility, they have two major drawbacks: they make accidental war more likely; and they give worse outcomes should deterrence fail. Responsible governments are, rightly, likely to depend on declared policy, rehearsed in exercises, with authority retained at the highest level, to give as convincing a posture as possible.

The credibility of a nuclear response is also increased as the number of independent nuclear weapon states increases. If more than one such state is threatened, then a lack of political will in one place can be compensated for by firmness in another. Multiple centres of independent decision-making increase the credibility of an alliance deterrent. The converse situation arises in an alliance when more than one state must agree before nuclear weapons can be used. In this case, a lack of will on the part of any of the chain of decision-making states would affect the response of them all; and thus the credibility of the deterrent posture of such an arrangement is reduced. 'Dual-key' nuclear systems may offer reassurance to the public, but they are not as effective as deterrent forces.

In discussing capability necessary to deter, the necessity for invulnerable retaliatory forces was highlighted earlier in this chapter. Not only must these forces be invulnerable but – of greater importance – the potential enemy must believe that they are. This can be done by making the problem of their simultaneous pre-emptive destruction as difficult as possible. Sheer numbers of systems compound the problem of their destruction. Different basing systems – submarine, air-launched, ground-based, ship-carried, low altitude transit and ballistic flight – all serve to complicate the attacker's disabling strike plan, and hence increase the credibility of the deterrent posture. The multiplication of weapon systems also acts as an insurance against future technological developments, which might render a particular basing system too vulnerable to retain credibility.

The final aspect of credibility is concerned with the potential aggressor's perception of the defender's areas of vital interest. A deterrent posture will fail if the potential enemy does not believe that it applies in a particular crisis. By failing to make an unambiguous security commitment to South Korea when their troops withdrew in 1949, the Americans could not expect their deterrent posture to be as effective as if they had given a guarantee. One study by George and Smoke[23] concludes that deterrence failed because the Communists did not believe Korea was an area of vital interest to the United States. The problem does not end with the defining and signalling of areas of vital interest. Future credibility depends on whether these areas are defended when necessary. A failure to meet an alliance or treaty obligation, or the appearance of a lack of resolve in one crisis, can reduce the overall credibility of a deterrent posture for the future.

In summary, credibility deals with mutual perceptions and cannot be an absolute science. A massive risk needs only to be slightly credible to deter; a less intimidating threat may by its nature be more credible, yet not deter as much.

RATIONALITY AND DETERRENCE

For deterrence to operate, a certain level of rationality must be presumed in the decision-making process of the state which is to be deterred. At minimum, this needs to be an assumption that the enemy will refrain from war if he believes that he will lose more, by going to war, than by refraining from war. It can be argued that the penalties of nuclear retaliation are so great that a form of rationality will be necessarily imposed on what may otherwise be a less than rational government. Professor Waltz has explored the question of whether, had nuclear weapons been available, Hitler's behaviour could have been moderated.

He concludes that Germany, either through Hitler or his generals, would have been deterred.[24] Even if this speculation were true, it is equally possible to postulate irrational enemies, nuclear terrorists for example, who would not be deterred. For those who lack the rationality to understand the rules of the game, deterrence theory has no answers.

When mutual deterrence is operating, similar assumptions must be made about the rationality of both sides. If these assumptions of rationality are followed through, an interesting paradox emerges. Kahn made the point, since made by many others:

> In most deterrence situations, once deterrence has failed, it is irrational to carry out the previously made warnings or threats of retaliation since that action will produce an absolute or net loss to the retaliator.[25]

If the carrying out of the threat is irrational, and there is an assumption of rationality, then the threat will not deter, and deterrence fails. Fortunately, the knot tied by these assumptions of consistent rationality is not difficult to cut through. Patrick Morgan summed up the problem as:

> The ultimate problem in devising a theory of deterrence is to simultaneously postulate that officials and governments are sometimes in some ways conscious and rational, yet take into account that certain forces work to make their behaviour unconscious and irrational.[26]

Governments cannot be aware of all the possible outcomes of any decision: they have less than perfect information, intellect and control; they are subject to conflicting pressures; and their alternatives may be constrained in different ways at different times. If deterrence were to fail, there is little prospect that an attacked nation would act in a purely rational way. Deterrence can operate because of the entirely rational fear that the opposition will act less than rationally, once it has suffered loss.

It is interesting to see how Bernard Brodie modified his views as a result of the success of nuclear deterrence. In 1959, he wrote:

Over the long term a policy of deterrence threatens to founder on the fact that too few people are sufficiently rational or sufficiently wise, with respect to either diplomacy or strategy to make it work.[27]

Fourteen years later he said:

It is a curious paradox of our time that one of the foremost factors making deterrence really work, and work well, is the lurking fear that in some massive confrontation crisis it might fail. Under these circumstances one does not tempt fate.[28]

The rationality paradox is solved by the understanding that it is entirely normal for human beings to act irrationally, especially when under pressure.

THE LIMITATIONS OF DETERRENCE THEORY

Deterrence theory has emerged through the work of social scientists, historians, scientists, military thinkers, politicians and the followers of many disciplines. It is by no means a cohesive internally consistent theory which can predict best strategies for every scenario. Indeed, some deductions are mutually exclusive. Nevertheless, it can show which factors may be of importance when attempting to make a deterrent posture more effective.

The examination of the requirements necessary to meet the four conditions for deterrence showed an edifice built on mutual perceptions and assessments of risk in an unpredictably rational world. While theory could point to ways to improve deterrence posture, the results often made the outcome, if deterrence failed, less controllable. The realities of the world can make the structure and strategy of the deterrent force quite different from the ideal. In Part II, this practical application of nuclear weapons to strategy is examined.

Part II

National Strategy

CHAPTER TWO

UNITED STATES' NUCLEAR STRATEGY

It is often assumed that the nuclear strategy of the United States is more easily codified than that of the USSR because of the much freer dissemination of information. While much has been written by analysts and advisers, and much has been said by both military men and politicians, the true nuclear strategy, planned or unplanned, can only be deduced by an examination of the overall targeting plan at any given time. It is tempting to suggest that a particular strategic doctrine was being implemented during a given period, and then to demonstrate how the military posture supported this doctrine; but this approach is less than honest. The development of new weapons may be in response to a change in strategy, but may also be the result of the pressures of industrial or military lobby groups, the momentum of research, or the inertia of the procurement organisation.

To examine the development of nuclear strategy in the United States, it is necessary to compare the capabilities with the declared policies in the light of the perceived threat.

NUCLEAR PRE-EMINENCE 1945-1950

When World War II ended, the United States found it prudent to build up a stockpile of atomic bombs. Any potential nuclear weapon state is limited by the time that it takes to produce weapons' grade fissile material. The American stockpile grew, even though there was no strategy in the immediate post-war period for the specific use of nuclear weapons. There was, however, sufficient concern about the future implications of such weapons for the Administration to push hard for the international control of all nuclear activities through the Baruch Plan. By 1948, the arsenal contained 50 atomic bombs, which could be delivered by a total of 32 suitably modified B-29s.[1] While the strategic thinkers, such as Bernard Brodie,[2] were announcing the advent of deterrence, the military were absorbing the new weapons into their contingency planning. Atomic bombs were seen as more effective aerial bombardment weapons, which could be employed in future conflicts to re-enact the strategic bombing of World War II with greater success.

The American perception for the threat of Communist expansion grew during the period. The Truman Doctrine, in 1947, formalised the opposition to the spread of Communism and by mid-1948, when the Soviets blockaded Berlin, war between the United States and the Soviet Union was an imminent possibility. The study by George and Smoke[3] concludes that the Blockade was an example of the failure of the American nuclear supremacy to deter lower level confrontations. It would seem as valid to suggest that it was the nuclear element which deterred sufficiently to keep the conflict at a low level.

NUCLEAR SUPERIORITY IN THE 1950s

The Soviet Union tested its first successful atomic device on 23 September 1949. This did not instantly make it capable of effective nuclear retaliation to any attack by the United States. It did, however, concentrate the minds of the planners to the prospect of a future where a nuclear strike might be reciprocated. Michael Mandelbaum describes the 'New Look' of the Eisenhower Administration in 1953 as the first time that the American government had given a formal answer to what political purposes atomic weapons would serve, and how they should be deployed to serve these purposes.[4]

The Secretary of State, John Foster Dulles, in a speech in 1954 stated that it was the aim of the United States to deter the

Soviets, by meeting a range of Communist acts of aggression with the full might of 'massive retaliation'. However by April, he had tempered this view slightly, and was saying:

> *In many cases any open assault by Communist forces could only result in starting a general war. But the Free World must have the means for responding effectively on a selective basis when it chooses.*[5]

The policy retained a degree of ambiguity: massive retaliation, with a flavour of flexible response to make it more digestible.

Professor Rathjens, who was involved with target planning, recalls that there were three types of strategic targets considered. These were the 'Bravo' against military targets in the Soviet Union; the 'Delta' destruction mission aimed at the Soviet war-making potential; and the 'Romeo' mission designed to retard the movement of Soviet forces into Western Europe. Discussion over priorities reveals the relative importance accorded to each:

> *As might have been expected, there was conflict over allocation or effort to the three missions: arguments about which allocation would have the most favourable effect on war outcome – significantly, not about whether allocating more resources to, say, the 'Delta' mission would enhance deterrence.*[6]

Aaron Friedberg confirms the wide range of targets during this period.[7] Despite the political debate over whether the policy of retaliation against the enemy's cities and industry was the right one, an increasing target list of Soviet military installations was being developed. However, while counter-force targeting might have its military (and moral) attraction, it was technically impractical because of the limited weapon accuracy.

MUTUAL ASSURED DESTRUCTION 1961-1974

Defence policy had played a significant part in the presidential election campaign of John F. Kennedy. It was inevitable that his coming into office, in January 1961, would be an occasion for a widescale review of American nuclear strategy. He had dwelt much on the forecast 'missile gap', which echoed the country's new realisation that it was from henceforwards directly vulnerable in war. He quickly made it clear that the policy of deterrence through massive retaliation was to be maintained. His Secretary of Defense, Robert S. McNamara, saw the problem initially as ensuring that the deterrent remained credible, even if the enemy could launch a pre-emptive attack. The policy must be to provide a survivable retaliatory force:

> We can no longer hope to have such a deterrent merely by maintaining a larger stockpile of nuclear weapons. Our weapons must be hardened, dispersed, and mobile so that they can survive an enemy attack ...[8]

In this speech in February 1962, McNamara elaborated how these survivable forces could be used. The single massive attack was one option. They could be used to 'limit damage to ourselves, and our allies, by knocking out the enemy's bases before he has time to launch his second salvos'. A third possible use was as a bargaining weapon to terminate a war. The new policy offered the flexibility to choose from several operational plans, without requiring any specific advance commitment. He emphasised the need to balance nuclear strength with adequate non-nuclear capability.

In June 1962, the strategy was considerably refined when McNamara said that the 'principal military objectives, in the events of a nuclear war stemming from a major attack on the Alliance, should be the destruction of the enemy's military forces, not of his civilian population'. He went on to indicate that the ability to destroy an enemy society would still be available, and that this would give 'the strongest imaginable incentive to refrain from striking our cities'.[9]

The Cuban missile crisis of October 1962 made the practical application of nuclear strategy an imminent possibility. Robert Kennedy writes of the attention which the President gave to every detail of both the diplomatic and the military aspects of the crisis.[10] From this, it seems inconceivable that, if nuclear weapons had been used, it would have been other than very selectively: individually and expressly approved by the President.

George and Smoke, in their analysis of the crisis, conclude that:

> *Thereafter, both sides substantially lowered their expectations regarding the extent to which deterrence and counter deterrence strategies could be used on behalf of foreign policy objectives.*[11]

In any event, the economic implications of a counter-force strategy, and the reluctance of the public to relish a war-fighting scenario, led the Administration to concentrate on the question of the size of nuclear forces, rather than on strategy. Thus in 1965, McNamara talked of the forces being required for two purposes: assured destruction and damage limitation. By quantifying the necessary level of assured destruction as 'say, one quarter to one third of its population and about two thirds of its industrial capacity', the required force could be calculated and defence expenditure restrained. He went on to explain the difficulty of the damage limiting role:

> *If we were to try to assure survival of a very high percentage of our population, and if the Soviets were to decide to frustrate this attempt because they viewed it as a threat to their assured destruction capability, the extra cost to them would appear to be substantially less than the extra cost to us.*[12]

McNamara's conversion from the invulnerable counter-force capability, with the reserve retaliatory force, was complete by 1967, when he stated that:

> *It is our ability to destroy an attacker as a viable 20th Century nation that provides the deterrent, not our ability to partially limit damage to ourselves.*[13]

A politician can announce a change of strategy in an instant; it takes rather longer for the military to turn new policy into operational practice. How did the Pentagon keep pace with the changes in priorities? The indications are that it continued unruffled by the changing doctrine. The decade had begun with the first attempt at overall coordination of nuclear targeting: the Single Integrated Operational Plan (SIOP) for the conduct of nuclear war. The first SIOP was an 'optimum mix' of military, industrial and government control targets, for use in a single massive attack. The revision of the SIOP in 1961, to meet the new counter-force requirement, distinguished between the three tasks of attacking nuclear threat targets, other military forces and urban/industrial targets. It also provided options for withholding attack from individual countries or from cities.[14] This was the strategic flexibility of which McNamara had spoken in his speech at Ann Arbor. He had also called upon NATO to 'strengthen further their non-nuclear forces'.[15] The strategy of strong conventional forces coupled with a wide range of nuclear options was to form the basis of the 'flexible response' concept.

At the strategic level, the target list increased as weapons became available, and no particular emphasis on city (massive retaliation) targets was given, as the Administration view swung back towards mutual assured destruction. The military targets were considered to be the most urgent, should war start, and so received the greater effort. While the cities were nominally the first priority, all that was required was a high level of confidence in the ability to destroy them. Theatre nuclear weapons were increasingly deployed in Europe, although firm Presidential control was retained through locking devices, known as Permissive Action Links (PALs).[16] No significant improvements in conventional forces were made.

The 1960s and early 1970s were characterised by the political realisation that a nuclear war could not be fought and won. The deterrent effect of mutual assured destruction must prevent the war. The credibility of massive retaliation was to be maintained by flexible response. That the forces and planning were not tailored to the concept was highlighted by President Nixon's dramatic question in 1970:

Should a President in the event of a nuclear attack be left
with the single option of ordering the mass destruction of

*enemy civilians, in the face of the certainty that it would
be followed by the mass slaughter of Americans?*[17]

Although he had rather more options than his rhetorical
question would suggest, the pre-planned flexible response
involved options each of which used large numbers of weapons.
In 1974, the Secretary of Defense, James R. Schlesinger,
admitted that this had been the case since 1961.[18]

LIMITED NUCLEAR OPTIONS 1974 ONWARDS

The credibility of a deterrent posture, which could involve the
total devastation of the United States of America in the defence
of Western Europe, was as questionable in 1974 as it had been
in 1961. The solution was again to develop some practical
options which would save the President from the stark choices
of surrender or suicide. The doctrine of flexible response had
not provided the practical options at the operational level. It
was accepted that deterrence might fail, and that the planning
must take that into account. In 1974, Secretary Schlesinger
made this clear:

*Deterrence can fail in many ways. What we need is a
series of measured responses to aggression which bear
some relation to the provocation, have prospects of
terminating hostilities before general nuclear war breaks
out, and leave some possibility for restoring deterrence.*[19]

At the same time, he emphasised the need to preserve the
ultimate sanction of massive retaliation, invulnerable at all
times. However, for lower levels of action, it was essential to
have a wide range of target options. These options must include
a capability for accurate attacks, with minimum collateral
damage. He also stated that the US would avoid any
combination of forces which might appear to the USSR to be
providing a first strike disarming capability.

From the military planning aspect, the new policy gave
authority to continue targeting military installations, nuclear
forces and urban/industrial centres as before. Technology was

providing greater accuracy of weapons, more warheads per missile, less vulnerability, shorter response time and greater quantities of battlefield information available to the commander (in theory). The new weapons, with their rapid retargeting facility, greater accuracy and range of warhead sizes, are well suited to a plan which requires many options. It is less certain whether the strategy generated the technology, or vice versa. In a recent study, Donald Snow concluded:

> *The simple fact, as has been suggested earlier, is that improved targeting accuracy has been an incremental outcome of guidance technology and, akin to MIRV, is a classic case of technology leading doctrine. Doctrinal rationalization and virtue have had to be developed after the fact, and, in all likelihood, no conscious a priori decision was ever made to try to attain a hard-target kill capability.*[20]

Certainly the balance of evidence seems to support this view of the development of American nuclear strategy.

The gradual transition to a formulation of a posture suited to the best outcome should deterrence fail was added to in 1977. Secretary of Defense Rumsfeld changed the emphasis of the massive retaliation mission to that of retarding the ability of the USSR to recover from a nuclear exchange and regain the status of a 20th century power more rapidly than the United States.[21] His successor, Harold Brown, voiced the concern that still existed over the range of crises which could be deterred by nuclear forces:

> *We no longer seriously believe (if we ever did) that we can credibly deter most hostile action by the threat of nuclear retaliation. Nuclear forces are useful primarily as a deterrent to nuclear actions and to overwhelming non-nuclear attacks.*[22]

The wide range of targets was confirmed by President Carter in his Presidential Directive 59 in July 1980. He directed that war planning should emphasise the effectiveness of attacks against military targets, although retaining the destruction of the Soviet economic and industrial base as a principal objective. The 'number and variety of options available to the President in the event of Soviet attack, at any level' were increased.[23]

Much of the same doctrinal ground had been covered in the 1960s as was covered in the 1970s. The new doctrine of limited nuclear options, was, in effect, flexible response with the appropriate weapons and operational plans. Doubts remained at the political level about the credibility of deterrence at lower levels. Doctrine in military circles centred on what to do if deterrence failed.

FUTURE TRENDS

The examination of American nuclear strategy over the past 36 years suggests that the analysts and politicians have made little headway out of the paradoxes of credible extended deterrence. The military capability has steadily increased, from the 50 atomic bombs of 1948 to the 10,000 weapons available today for the 40,000 targets of SIOP-5.[24] The consistent thread throughout the period has been the securing of an invulnerable massive retaliation capability. The submarine force is likely to provide this capability into the future; barring an unexpected breakthrough in either anti-submarine warfare, or anti-ballistic missile defence.

The Reagan Administration made the modernisation of nuclear forces the major factor in its defence policy. Defense Secretary Caspar Weinberger expressed the rationale as:

> *The specific objectives of President Reagan's program are to regain and to maintain the strategic balance with the Soviet Union, where balance is the key to deterring any attack by them against ourselves or our allies.*[25]

This doctrine of deterrence through balance, rather than through specific capabilities, reflects a prevalent feeling that relative numbers are psychologically important. Among the new developments which Weinberger outlined, he made a particular point of the requirement for an improvement in accuracy of the land-based missiles. This is probably another instance of technology determining policy, but it has generated considerable criticism. Greater accuracy is of use for strategic missiles if they are to be aimed at the enemy's hardened missile silos. As there is limited value in destroying empty silos, and the land-based missiles are themselves vulnerable to attack, the critics see the new proposals as being directed at the development of a first strike force, which they believe is destabilising.

In 1983, President Reagan announced a new direction in strategic thinking:

> *Let me share with you a vision of the future which offers hope. It is, that we embark on a program to counter the awesome Soviet missile threat with measures that are defensive ... What if free people could live secure in the knowledge that their security did not rest upon the threat of instant US retaliation to deter a Soviet attack; we could intercept and destroy strategic ballistic missiles before they reached our own soil or that of our allies?[26]*

This desire for a policy based on strategic defence echoes back to McNamara's search for a damage limitation strategy in the early 1960s. The technological, financial, tactical and strategic questions which need to be answered make it still an uncertain venture. The President's own Commission on Strategic Forces remains sceptical:

> *At this time, however, the Commission believes that no ABM technologies appear to combine practicality, survivability, low-cost and technical effectiveness sufficiently to justify proceeding beyond the stage of technology development.[27]*

In summary, the politicians have throughout the period tried to find ways to make nuclear deterrence credible for all levels of conflict by various declaratory postures. The military have evolved their plans for action should deterrence fail. The scientists have produced weapons with the traditional military improvements of accuracy, range, reliability, effectiveness, flexibility and invulnerability. The sum has been to produce a force, greatly in excess of any massive retaliation requirement, but one of such power that it is difficult to conceive of an enemy taking the risk of unleashing it.

CHAPTER THREE

SOVIET NUCLEAR STRATEGY

Much has been written in the West about the overall strategy of the Soviet Union for the employment of its nuclear weapons. An analysis of the public pronouncements of the leaders of a closed society, the unclassified military manuals, the editorials of the state controlled press, and the writings of dissidents is unlikely to provide the complete picture. Experts in the West are unable to agree about such basic points as the future military intentions of the Soviet Union: whether they are offensive or defensive.

While it may not be possible to determine their intentions, it is possible to draw broad conclusions on Soviet philosophy for the use of nuclear weapons, from their force structure both now and in the past.

STALIN AND NUCLEAR INFERIORITY

The decision to build the Soviet atomic bomb was taken in the summer of 1942.[1] The Soviet reaction to the Baruch Plan for the international control of atomic weapons in 1946 ensured that it would fail. Stalin saw the turmoil at the end of World War II as an opportunity for expanding the Communist empire. The forces of the United States and Western Europe had been massively demobilised, while the Soviet forces had not. Stalin's major test of the resolve of the West was the Berlin Blockade in 1948. That he chose not to use his superior conventional strength and tactical position suggests a concern for nuclear vulnerability.

The Soviet strategy for the period when it had no strategic nuclear capability appears to have been one of exploiting advantageous but low risk situations. It was not prepared to risk a full scale conflict with a United States which could use nuclear weapons with impunity. The large conventional forces must be kept in being while the nuclear capability was developed. The first successful test of an atomic device took place on 23 September 1949.

KHRUSHCHEV AND STRATEGIC CAPABILITY

By 1955, Nikita Khrushchev had emerged as the major figure of the Soviet leadership. At the same time, they were at last gaining a strategic nuclear capability, which, however inferior, they were prepared to brandish. Bulganin told Eden of Britain's vulnerability to attack using 'rocket technique' should Britain continue the Suez operation.[2] While the British may not have taken this threat seriously in 1956, the launch of Sputnik the following year made the world realise the new strategic capabilities of the Soviet Union.

Khrushchev made it absolutely clear that he considered the nuclear strategic missile to be the cornerstone of his military policy. In his statement to the Supreme Soviet in 1960, he proposed reducing the armed forces by 1,200,000 men and disposing of military aviation and surface ships. The strategic rocket forces would make the current structure unnecessary:

In our time a country's defence capacity is determined not by the number of soldiers it has under arms, the number of men in uniform. Aside from the general political and economic factors about which I have already spoken, a country's defence capacity depends to a decisive extent upon the firepower and the means of delivery it has.[3]

Although some reductions were made, the opposition of the military establishment and the Berlin and Cuba crises prevented Khrushchev from fulfilling his aim. There is little doubt that he considered the strategic rocket forces to be an overwhelming deterrent to external aggression. Hannes

Adomeit concludes that Khrushchev deduced the effectiveness of deterrence from the lack of retribution in August 1961, following the building of the Berlin Wall. This then encouraged him to attempt to present a second *fait accompli* in Cuba, having resumed weapon testing as a forceful reminder of Soviet capabilities.[4] If this analysis is correct, as seems possible, then the Soviet strategy was one of opportunistic action under the cover of nuclear retaliatory threat. The military view differed greatly from the political doctrine of the overriding importance of nuclear fire-power over manpower. Many leading figures of the Soviet military establishment made clear their belief in the need for a grand war-fighting capability.[5]

BREZHNEV AND NUCLEAR PARITY

Following the fall of Khrushchev in 1964, the military view of the need for strong conventional forces coupled with strong nuclear forces prevailed. It is evident that achieving parity with the United States was the first priority. By the start of the Strategic Arms Limitation Talks (SALT) in Helsinki in late 1969, the Soviet Union had agreed with the United States on the existence of and the need to preserve parity, mutual deterrence and strategic stability.[6] In fact, because of delays to the SALT process as a result of the invasion of Czechoslovakia in 1968, when the agreement was made the numbers of launchers permitted gave the Soviets a numerical superiority in this area.

The agreements to arms limitations did not mean that the Soviets accepted the American concept of mutual assured destruction. The Soviet military writings, the political statements and the force structure all appear to be internally consistent with the view that nuclear weapons are seen as an essential part of the preparations for war. Joseph Douglass, in his *Soviet Strategy for Nuclear War*, draws extensively on the classified organ of the Soviet General Staff, *'Voyennaya mysl'*, which was passed to the West by Penkovsky. Quotes from this source give an indication of the development of current Soviet strategy:

The most important task of the General Staff in preparing for modern war is the detailed employment of nuclear weapons by all services of the armed forces.
(Major General N. Komkov, October 1964)[7]

For the achievement of victory in a present-day nuclear war, if it is unleashed by the imperialists, not only the enemy's armed forces, but also the sources of his military power and state control as well as areas where different branches of the armed forces are based, will be subjected to simultaneous destruction.
(Colonel M. Shirokov April 1968)[8]

In view of the immense destructive force of nuclear weapons and the extremely limited time available to take effective countermeasures after an enemy launches its missiles, the launching of the first massed attack acquires decisive importance for achieving the objectives of war.
(Marshal of the Soviet Union K. Moshalenko January 1969)[9]

These writings from closed circulation journals do not differ in philosophy from open publications. The policy is further confirmed by the force structure. The strategic rocket forces form a separate arm of the armed forces; active defence against air attack is widely deployed; and civil defence measures have been widely implemented. Irrespective of the effectiveness of these measures, the resources devoted to them show that the Soviet view of deterrence is significantly different from the American one. It is usually described as 'deterrence by denial', rather than the West's doctrine of deterrence by punishment.[10] The demonstrated capability and willingness to fight a nuclear war, and hence deny a victory to the enemy, acts as the deterrent to aggression. What we can glean of their targeting doctrine from quotations, such as those of Colonel Shirokov above, is that it is entirely counter-force. That large cities will contain points of 'military and state control', ensures that the collateral damage would be as great as that from a counter-value targeting doctrine.

It does not necessarily follow, as is sometimes suggested, that a force posture and doctrine for nuclear war fighting means that the Soviets believe they can use nuclear war as an instrument of policy, or could win, in any meaningful sense, an all out nuclear war. Robert Arnett, after studying Soviet pronouncements, concludes that they are acutely aware of the American capability to inflict unacceptable damage.[11] The doctrine of fighting a war, rather than mutual vulnerability, is necessary both for ideological reasons, and for morale, especially in the military.

If they do not believe that their nuclear forces can be sensibly used to achieve a victory, then why did they engage on the massive build up in the second half of the 1960s, and why the comprehensive modernisation programme in progress now? Professor Erickson identifies three possible explanations for the first expansion.[12] Firstly, it could have been an attempt to achieve stability through parity. Secondly, it may have been an attempt to achieve strategic advantage as part of a master plan. The third possibility, which he favours, is that it proceeded without any well defined single objective, as a result of the various institutional pressures and interests at work within the Soviet system. Brian Crozier strongly favours the master plan concept, and quotes a leaked intelligence report of Brezhnev's address to the East European communist leaders in 1973.[13] At this meeting, Brezhnev is said to have spoken of a decisive shift in the correlation of forces, such that by 1985, they could exert their will whenever they needed to.

Whatever the true motives, the Soviet armoury is entirely logical in their terms. They may not want a nuclear war, but they realise that it could happen. In that event, they would wish to limit the damage to themselves, and would also wish to emerge as the most powerful of the survivors. To this end an offensive war-waging capability, which is superior to the potential enemy, is a logical posture. Active and passive defences improve prospects of recovery.

The Soviet strategy differs from the American in how a nuclear war is likely to be conducted, should deterrence fail. The early use of decisive fire-power is basic to the doctrine; and the relatively high dependence on vulnerable land-based ICBMs suggests that they would be used in a first strike, or in a launch on warning role. Certainly the NATO concept of an escalating limited nuclear war is totally discounted:

> *As a matter of fact, there can be in general no 'limited' nuclear war. If a nuclear war breaks out, whether it be in Europe or in any other place, it would inevitably and unavoidably assume a worldwide character ... So, those who possibly hope to set fire to the nuclear powder-keg, while themselves sitting to one side, should not entertain any illusions.*
>
> (L.I. Brezhnev)[14]

The American proposals of a change of strategy to strategic defence is no more welcome to the Soviet leadership:

> *Should this conception be converted into reality, this would actually open the floodgates of a runaway race of all types of strategic arms, both offensive and defensive. Such is the real purport, the seamy side, so to say, of Washington's 'Defensive conception'.*
>
> (Y. Andropov)[15]

FUTURE TRENDS

It is difficult to imagine any radical change in Soviet nuclear strategy, especially while the old guard retain the reigns of power. It has been remarkably consistent and, some might suggest, more successful at instilling fear in its enemies than the American strategy in recent years. Paul Nitze has suggested six main Soviet objectives for the 1980s: the separation of NATO Europe from the US; increase of influence in the Persian Gulf; encirclement and neutralisation of China; subversion in the West, particularly the Caribbean; ability to deal with direct East/West military confrontation if necessary; and finally, the improvement of the Soviet image as a responsible participant of the international community.[16] An increasing conventional and nuclear superiority, to give deterrence by denial, and a damage limiting doctrine should deterrence fail, would not be at variance with these aims.

CHAPTER FOUR

BRITISH NUCLEAR STRATEGY

Scientific research in Britain, and in particular the work of the Maud Committee in 1940 and 1941, had demonstrated the feasibility of the uranium isotope, U^{235} atomic bomb, and the possibility of the plutonium bomb. The report gave an added impetus to research in the United States and a fully collaborative venture was in being by 1943. Britain was, therefore, totally involved in the original development of atomic weapons. There was a natural assumption that, as a great power and victor of the war, Britain would continue to take a leading role in atomic energy research and development after 1945.

The new Labour government was only a week old when the Hiroshima bomb was dropped on 6 August 1945. Margaret Gowing has written a comprehensive exposition of the decision-making processes which led to the British atomic bomb.[1] Although no decision to produce an atomic bomb was taken initially, the Cabinet sub-committee, GEN 75, set up a research establishment at Harwell tasked with investigating all aspects of atomic energy. It soon became clear that the Americans had no intention of sharing the fruits of their own atomic research, and in August 1946, the McMahon Act made the exchange of all such information illegal.

Although there was no political decision to produce atomic weapons, the military were convinced of the need to have an atomic capability to match any other power which might develop such weapons. At the end of 1945, the Chiefs of Staff were pressing for two atomic piles to be built, as they would need as many atomic bombs as possible.[2] In August 1946, the Chief of the Air Staff put in a demand through normal procurement channels for an atomic bomb.[3] The political decision to proceed was taken in January 1947. The bomb was developed quite independently of the United States, and successfully tested on 3 October 1952. It was assumed that the build up of nuclear stockpiles in America and Russia would be comparatively slow, and that the British force would therefore be of major significance in deterring the use of Soviet bombs against the British isles.[4]

INCREASING RELIANCE ON THE NUCLEAR THREAT

The 1952 Chiefs of Staff Global Strategy Paper argued that more reliance should be placed on nuclear threats to contain Soviet expansion.[5] The nuclear arsenal was seen as the counter to the Soviet conventional force superiority. It was not until 1956 that Britain had a significant operational nuclear capability with the coming into service of the V-bomber force. The dependence on the effectiveness of this force was such that the following year, the Defence White Paper stated that large conventional forces would no longer be necessary.[6] The 800,000 men in the armed forces in 1956 were to be reduced to 375,000 by 1962. The 1958 Defence White Paper made it clear that the nuclear deterrent forces were the mainstay of defence:

> *In fact, the strategy of NATO is based on the frank recognition that a full-scale Soviet attack could not be repelled without resort to a massive nuclear bombardment of the sources of power in Russia.*[7]

There was a complete reliance on a massive retaliation strategy as a response to Soviet aggression; and Britain was the first country to base its national defence upon a declared policy of nuclear deterrence.[8] The potential vulnerability of the aircraft delivery system, even with the stand-off Blue Steel glide bomb, was recognised. A ballistic missile, Blue Streak, was therefore to be developed. It was cancelled in 1960, when it was appreciated that the likely cost of £600 million would eventually provide an obsolete system, which, because of liquid fuelling and soft launchers, would be vulnerable to surprise attack. America was prepared to supply an air-launched ballistic missile system, Skybolt, which was under development and could be used by the V-bombers. On 7 November 1962, the United States announced the cancellation of the Skybolt programme. Technical problems and the vulnerability of aircraft-based systems made the Minuteman and Polaris much more attractive prospects to them. Prime Minister Macmillan salvaged the situation by obtaining an extremely advantageous agreement from President Kennedy, at Nassau in December 1962, for the supply of Polaris to Britain. An American technical and economic decision was therefore responsible for the radical change in the basis of the British deterrent: Polaris could have been opted for in 1960 if it had been preferred to Skybolt.[9]

THE CONTRIBUTION TO NATO

The Nassau agreement formalised the assignment of the British nuclear forces to NATO, and brought them into the American nuclear targeting plan. Macmillan insisted on preserving the option for independent use in the supreme national interest. This independence clause may have been predominantly to preserve Britain's great power role; but France was already expressing concern over the credibility of the American nuclear support for Europe, and this may have been a factor. In 1964, the Defence White Paper did consider the possibility of a 'mistaken' Soviet belief in the unwillingness of America to defend Europe, and hence the need for a European nuclear power.[10]

The Labour government of 1964 played down the independent aspect of Britain's nuclear forces. The 1965 Defence Estimates centred on the contribution to NATO and the proposed, but never to be formed, Atlantic Nuclear Force. The only reference to possible independent use was in relation to the Chinese atomic test, and the ability of the British nuclear force to provide some reassurance to non-nuclear powers.[11] The lack of direction in British nuclear strategy was expressed in an Editorial of the *Royal United Services Institute Journal* in 1966, to mark the launching of HMS *Resolution*, the first of the Polaris submarines:

> *The political background to Polaris has been more troubled than the background to what one might call the purely hardware side, mainly because there is no authoritative statement of what the British Polaris fleet is expected to achieve.*[12]

The emergence of the doctrine of flexible response in the United States in the early 1960s was not greeted with great enthusiasm by Britain. A strategy which called for more conventional forces and greater manpower was not economically attractive. When the doctrine was adopted as official NATO policy in 1967, the British Army was some 191,000 strong; virtually half its size ten years before. The size has not subsequently increased, and therefore Britain uses fewer conventional forces when following a strategy of graduated response than when it adhered to a massive retaliation policy.

THE SECOND DECISION CENTRE

The unwillingness of Britain and the other European NATO countries greatly to enhance their conventional capabilities meant that, notwithstanding flexible response, the American strategic nuclear guarantee remained the basis of the security of Western Europe. Yet as North America became more and more vulnerable to the Soviet strategic arsenal, this guarantee became less credible. In this dilemma, the British deterrent had a new role to play. Defence Minister, Denis Healey has been credited with first postulating the 'second centre for decision making' strategy in 1964.[13] Through the 1970s, this concept was used in official statements about nuclear forces, and in the 1980 Open Government Document discussing the choice of the Polaris replacement, it was the major consideration:

If Britain is to meet effectively the deterrent purpose of providing a second centre of decision-making within the alliance, our force has to be visibly capable of posing a massive threat on its own.[14]

The philosophy of this doctrine was explained by the Defence Minister, Francis Pym, as follows:

The decision to use nuclear weapons would be an agonising one for any national leadership and the Soviets must know this; but to have to calculate whether either of two powers would be prepared to do so if pressed to the extremity, doubles their uncertainty, complicates their planning and increases their risks. It is in this way that our strategic and theatre nuclear forces contribute so much to the collective deterrence of the Alliance.[15]

FUTURE TRENDS

The decision to replace the Polaris fleet with Trident, combined with NATO Theatre Nuclear Forces modernisation proposals, resulted in considerable public debate in Britain over nuclear strategy. The Labour party, in opposition, adopted the unilateral nuclear disarmament of Britain as policy at its 1980 conference, and stated in its 1983 election manifesto:

Labour's commitment is to establish a non-nuclear defence policy for this country. This means the rejection of any fresh nuclear bases or weapons on British soil or in British waters, and the removal of all existing nuclear bases and weapons, thus enabling us to make a direct contribution to an eventually much wider nuclear-free zone in Europe.[16]

Another rationale for the independent nuclear force is in the process of emerging. The replacement for Polaris will be operating well into the next century, by which time there may be many new lesser nuclear weapon states, and old alliances may have changed radically. In this unknown future, Defence Minister John Nott argued that Britain must have its own invulnerable deterrent force, to secure the country against any nuclear threat.[17] The British electorate appeared to support this view, and returned the Conservative Government.

CHAPTER FIVE

FRENCH NUCLEAR STRATEGY

THE FOURTH REPUBLIC

Although French scientists had been involved in early work on the development of the atomic bomb, France – like Britain – had no prospect of sharing in the fruits of American research after the war. The trauma of occupation made the re-establishment of France as a major power within a secure Europe the great concern of post-war governments. While the formation of NATO was welcomed as an aid to security, there was considerable debate in 1949 as to the credibility of the Anglo-Saxon guarantees to the European mainland.[1] The French military were well aware of the importance of atomic weapons, and much emphasis was placed on the tactics of the nuclear battlefield. This concern over the effect of atomic weapons on war tactics led to the emergence of a body of military opinion which considered them an essential part of the nation's arsenal. From the mid-1950s, this military view, coupled with the establishment hope that atomic weapons could give more strength per franc, formed a climate of opinion for the production of such weapons which could survive the changing governments.

While the government of the day did examine the question of producing atomic bombs from time to time, the decision was always postponed. As in Britain, research continued unhampered by political decision. The *Commissariat à l'Energie Atomique* (CEA) had been set up by General de Gaulle in October 1945 with similar broad terms of reference to those of Harwell. The CEA was entrusted with the mission of developing the uses of atomic energy for science, industry and national defence.[2] The initial period of research was followed by an industrial phase from 1952, which involved the construction of two plutonium producing reactors. In this way, the weapons production option was retained. The weapon development phase emerged in the mid-1950s, without any specific government decision having been taken. A study of how this happened concludes that:

> *Guidance and direction for nuclear policy came not from the French Government or the French Parliament, but from a small dedicated group of administrator-techno-crats, politicians and military officers, whose activities centred on and emanated from the CEA.*[3]

Through the changing coalition governments, the question of nuclear weapon development was raised at various times in the French parliament. A general understanding emerged that France was researching towards an eventual nuclear weapon capability. The Suez crisis of 1956 reinforced the mistrust of American protection, and a new CEA/National Defense protocol was signed, which formally established a five year military programme. The decision to prepare for the first French atomic test was not taken until April 1958 by Premier Gaillard. This was no more than a rubber stamp decision by another of the succession of weak governments.

THE DE GAULLE ERA

What coherent policy discussion that there had been during the Fourth Republic suggested that the role seen for atomic weapons was as a part of the NATO Alliance, albeit as an independent great power. The advent of Charles de Gaulle and the Fifth Republic changed this. After an early attempt to wrest the control of NATO from the United States by a change to tripartite control, de Gaulle declared his position at a speech at the *Ecole Militaire* on 3 November 1959. Having dismissed the NATO concept of integrated forces, he went on to say:

... what we must achieve during the coming years is a force capable of acting exclusively on our behalf, a force which has been conveniently called a 'force de frappe' susceptible to deployment anywhere at any time. It goes without saying that the basis for such a force will be atomic armament – whether we manufacture it or buy it – but one which belongs to us.[4]

There was little discussion of the strategy or force structure necessary. Kohl suggests that the aims of de Gaulle in producing the *force de frappe* were: the restoration of French grandeur, the reunification of Europe, the subordination of West Germany and hence French leadership in Europe, and ultimately an independent role for Europe in the world.[5]

On 13 February 1960, France successfully tested its first atomic bomb. Later that year, the government introduced its first five year plan for the development of national defence. The plan was concerned with nuclear weapons research and the procurement of both aircraft and missile delivery systems. In 1963, the first of the supersonic Mirage IV prototypes was delivered, and 50 were operational by 1966.[6] The arrival of the hardware of nuclear warfare might have been expected to lead to greater debate over nuclear strategy in the country. De Gaulle's interest in such academic matters appeared to be limited. He saw the nuclear force primarily as a diplomatic tool. His strategy is usually described as that of 'proportional deterrence'. He explained this in 1964:

Doubtless the megatons that we could launch would not equal in number those that the Americans and Russians are able to unleash. But once reaching a certain nuclear capability, and with regard to one's own direct defence, the proportion of respective means has no absolute value. Indeed, since a man and a people can only die once, the deterrent exists provided that one has the means to wound the possible aggressor mortally, that one is very determined to do it and that the aggressor is convinced of it.[7]

The French posture was one of immediate and massive

retaliation, once French territory was threatened. The concept of flexible response was rejected on the grounds that Europe would be destroyed as the host to the battle. The leading strategic thinkers in France in the 1960s were Generals Gallois and Beaufre. The former strongly resisted the concept of tactical nuclear weapons and their use for graduated deterrence, and the latter highlighted the importance of the second decision centre, which improved the overall credibility of the NATO deterrent. One official publication[8] reflected this view of deterrence enhanced through the uncertainty caused by independent decision centres.

Under de Gaulle, the nuclear strategy was completely interwoven with foreign policy. Up to 1962, he looked for power within the Western Alliance, and nuclear independence was the method of achieving this. From 1962 to 1965, he sought an independent position to deprive the Americans of control over the destiny of France. This was reflected in the concern over flexible response and multilateral force proposals. From 1965 until the invasion of Czechoslovakia in 1968, the French cultivated a very independent foreign policy. A nuclear strategy of *tous azimuths* was propounded, in which France must be prepared for attacks from any direction. General Ailleret argued that to meet unknown alliances of the future, France would need to build a completely independent defence system, which would include a significant number of long range strategic missiles.[9]

The invasion of Czechoslovakia by the Soviets brought an improvement to French-NATO relationships and a change in the declared nuclear strategy. The new Chief of Staff, General Fourquet, dropped all reference to *tous azimuths*, and made it clear that the threat was once more perceived as being from the Soviets. It is likely that financial constraints also influenced the decision to drop the long range missile programme. Some reappraisal of the instant massive retaliation strategy also took place. This was necessary to assign a role to the newly developed tactical nuclear weapons, and may have been a case of technology determining doctrine. Fourquet described the new strategy as one in which the tactical nuclear weapons would have the task of testing the enemy's intention and demonstrating France's will.

*Deterrence must be equally manifested at all conceivable
stages of combat so that our will to resist any aggression
appears quite clear, and marks our determination to have,
if necessary, rapid and inevitable recourse to the ultimate
weapon.*[10]

This was acceptance of flexible response, albeit with fewer
rungs on the escalation ladder and a lower nuclear threshold. It
raised a number of problems in relations with NATO, given
that such tactical weapons would need to be used against an
enemy in West Germany.

AFTER DE GAULLE

In France, the credibility of the nuclear deterrent was little
questioned. The force was never large, was vulnerable on the
ground, and the survivability of the Mirage IV was suspect
after 1969. The 1965 plan had recognised this by planning for
an intermediate range ballistic missile force, based on land, and
a submarine-based force. Financial constraints and difficulties
in development resulted in delays and cutbacks. It was not until
1971 that the first submarine, *Le Redoutable*, became
operational, with 18 land-based missiles coming the following
year. Yet the charisma of General de Gaulle had made the *force
de frappe* a credible deterrent up to 1969.

President Pompidou sought a strategy which could combine
the requirement for an effective force with the need for
economic restraint. He did, however, instigate a review for the
improvement of the armed forces in general, and the navy in
particular. The 1971-75 programme recognised the need to
improve conventional strength. President Giscard d'Estaing
also initiated a review in 1974, with a view to improving
conventional forces. He confirmed his belief in the doctrine of
proportional deterrence and said, 'France is and must remain
the third nuclear power in the world and it goes without saying
that we reject any idea of a ceiling on the French nuclear
force'.[11] His 1977-82 plan noted the depletion of conventional
forces, which had suffered at the expense of nuclear forces since
1960. The trend would be reversed, although the weapons yield

of the nuclear element would be quadrupled during the period.[12] An extra regiment of Pluton short range nuclear missiles was authorised, and the intermediate range – S2 – missiles are being replaced with the more powerful S3 version. A sixth submarine, *L'Inflexible*, was authorised, and is due into service in 1985.[13]

The increasing vulnerability of the land-based and aircraft elements of the French deterrent is evident. To compensate for the increased vulnerability to a first strike on the land-based missiles, the President announced in 1980 the intention to develop a mobile missile system for the 1990s.[14] The Mitterrand Socialist government has placed an increased emphasis on nuclear forces at the expense of conventional weapons. The 1984–88 programme devotes some 30 per cent of the equipment budget to nuclear systems. The French are willing to devote considerable resources to the maintenance of a fully independent nuclear force. The plans for the next decade are completely consistent with those of the past. They belie the commentator who said, 'French defense budgeting is similar to the British process in that strategic policy goals are less important in the fulfillment of equipment programs than financial constraints ...'[15] General Gallois remains contemptuous of extended deterrence and nuclear war-fighting, and believes that while the rest of NATO becomes more vulnerable to first strike attack, France retains a credible nuclear retaliatory response to any attack on its territory. 'The posture is the only appropriate one for a country like France that can only be on the defensive'.[16]

CHAPTER SIX

CHINESE NUCLEAR STRATEGY

Until as recently as the early 19th century, China was accustomed to its traditional role as the Asian power. For 2,000 years, China had seen itself as the 'middle kingdom': the centre of culture, influence and power. The collapse of the Chinese empire, the intervention of the European powers and the Communist revolution have not necessarily changed the traditional perception that the Chinese have of their world role. In 1943, Chiang Kai-shek, when speaking of the imposition on China of unequal treaties, said:

> *The people as a whole must regard this as a national humiliation, and not until all lost territories have been recovered can we relax our efforts to wipe out this humiliation and save ourselves from destruction.*[1]

Professor Liu has drawn attention to the similarity of the views of both the Nationalist and the Communist leaders in this respect. Mao Tse-tung was equally bitter about the many dependent states and parts of its territories which China had lost to the imperialist powers. Both leaders recognised the traditional superiority of China, and anticipated its future return to great power status.[2] Nevertheless, the advent of a Communist government has meant that ideology, rather than nationalism, is the declared driving force of foreign policy. An examination of nuclear strategy must bear in mind the undercurrent of the great power tradition.

CHINA WITHOUT NUCLEAR WEAPONS 1949-1963

Mao Tse-tung refused to acknowledge the importance of atomic weapons. There was, however, no doubt that China expected to get the technology, if not the bombs, from the Soviets. In 1953, the Committee of Atomic Energy was set up in the Chinese Academy of Science. In 1955, the Soviet Union announced that it would help China to study the peaceful uses of atomic energy, and would provide a research reactor. Two years later, the 'New Technology for National Defence' agreement was signed, and in 1958, the first experimental reactor came on line. The following year, the Soviets withdrew their assistance and the Chinese were later to claim that this broke a promise, given by the Soviets, that they would provide China with a sample atomic bomb.[3] It has been suggested[4] that the original Soviet aid was provided to buy unity in the Communist world, and subsequently delayed, in the hope that a Test Ban Treaty would stop China from producing a bomb.

During this period, the Chinese leaders both advocated general nuclear disarmament and also declared nuclear proliferation to be desirable. The rationale for these apparently conflicting policies was that either would break the nuclear monopoly of the United States and the Soviet Union. On proliferation they said:

> *Whether or not nuclear weapons help peace depends on who possesses them. It is detrimental to peace if they are in the hands of imperialist countries; it helps peace if they are in the hands of socialist countries. It must not be said undiscriminatingly that the danger of nuclear war increases along with the increase in the number of nuclear powers.*[5]

MAO'S MINIMUM DETERRENT 1964-1976

The withdrawal of support by the Soviet Union in 1959 may have slowed the Chinese nuclear programme. It has been suggested that Khrushchev personally made the decision, based on the suspicions of the independent course of the Chinese missile development.[6] It is a measure of the importance which Mao attached to the programme that as early as 16 October 1964, they tested their first static 20 kt atomic device. They rapidly increased yields, and reduced size, and by the test of 17 June 1967, they had exploded a thermonuclear device of 3 to 7 MT. The tests in 1965 and 1966 had included live aircraft and missile delivery respectively.[7] The three years from first atomic test to first thermonuclear test compares with eight years for the United States, five years for Great Britain and four years for the Soviet Union. Those working on both the weapons and the delivery systems development must have been exempted from the excesses of the Great Proletarian Cultural Revolution which began in September 1965.

Having successfully broken the nuclear monopoly, China seemed less enthusiastic about the prospect of proliferation. Vice-Premier Chen Yi in talking about nuclear cooperation with other countries, said in 1965, '... as for the request for China's help in the manufacture of atom bombs, this question is not realistic'.[8] Although China refuses to sign the Non-Proliferation Treaty, there is no evidence that the official view has changed since the policy expressed by Chen Yi. It has also been necessary to accommodate the possession of nuclear weapons with the policy of nuclear disarmament. To explain the position, Premier Chou En-lai wrote to heads of government on the day following the first test:

> The Chinese Government consistently stands for the complete prohibition and thorough destruction of nuclear weapons. China has been compelled to conduct nuclear testing and develop nuclear weapons. China's mastering of nuclear weapons is entirely for defence and for protecting the Chinese people from the US threat. The Chinese Government solemnly declares that at no time and in no circumstance will China be the first to use nuclear weapons.[9]

As China did not test its first intercontinental ballistic missile until as recently as 1980, this nuclear strategy of protecting

China from the United States is difficult to follow. Yet the stated policy was to bring nuclear retaliation to the American homeland. In 1965 the Defence Minister said:

> *US imperialism relies solely on its nuclear weapons to intimidate people. But these weapons cannot save US imperialism from its doom ... If it threatens other countries with nuclear weapons, US imperialism will expose its own country to the same threat.*[10]

The 29 issues of the secret Chinese military journal, *Kung-tso T'unghsun*, which were acquired by the United States government give some insight into the more realistic top level thinking in the Chinese military in the early 1960s. Hsieh concludes, from an examination of these journals, that Chinese thinking about war with the United States was entirely defensive.[11] They expected an American initiated attack as a 'bolt from the blue', with nuclear, biological and chemical weapons. They realised their vulnerability for the next three to five years, but they could still live to fight another day. A leading member of the Military Affairs Committee, Marshal Yeh Chien-ying said:

> *The objective in a war is primarily to annihilate the enemy, but attention should also be paid to the theme of self preservation. Particularly under the present circumstances, weapons causing casualties on a large scale and mass destruction have appeared in use. We cannot annihilate our enemy unless we pay enough attention to the preservation of our lives and strengths. We should not only prepare ourselves against the use of such weapons by our enemy in a sudden attack, but also safeguard ourselves from disaster when we ourselves employ them.*[12]

In addition to the deterrence of American attacks, nuclear weapons were also seen as a means of encouraging those peoples who were engaged in revolutionary wars. A number of the nuclear tests were accompanied by statements similar to this one of 9 May 1966, following the third test explosion: 'The Chinese people's possession of nuclear weapons is a great encouragement to the peoples who are fighting heroically for their own liberation'.[13] It is unlikely that the Chinese intended any direct application of their tiny nuclear forces to revolutionary wars; but the rhetoric may have been aimed at making the American nuclear guarantee less credible to pro-Western states in Asia. As the stockpile of weapons increased, the statements accompanying each test became more specific. After the tenth test, a three megaton bomb on 20 September 1969, the statement specified 'encouragement and support' given by Chinese nuclear weapons to the Vietnamese, the Laotians and the Palestinians, and to the people of all countries who are fighting for the people's liberation.[14]

It is difficult to postulate a consistent nuclear strategy through Mao's time, given the internal turmoil of 1966 and 1967, the widening rift with the Soviets, and the eventual rapprochement with the United States in 1972. Richard Nixon saw the warming of relations with America coming from the increasing concern about China's potentially hostile neighbours: Russia, India and Japan.[15] Gelber saw the Chinese as having five objectives: national security; regaining the lost great power status; extending influence in Asia; regaining lost territories; and leadership of the Communist world.[16] One can draw a number of parallels with the French view of nuclear strategy, if this was the case. He went on to describe how, as a lesser nuclear power sharing a common frontier with Russia, and possibly in conflict with either it or America, China has cultivated a strategy of 'strategic ambiguity': leaving everyone uncertain as to their strategy. There is much to support his view that:

There is no evidence that Peking considers these matters principally in terms of scenario writing, or that the usefulness of a Chinese force need depend on precisely formulated strategic purposes.[17]

AFTER MAO

The Chinese nuclear strategy after the death of Mao in 1976 was not made any clearer by the internal power struggles which took place. Test explosions continued, with a record four in one year in 1976, but there have been none reported since 1980. Rocket development has also continued. However, there seems to be no urgency in deploying operational forces. The force of less than 150 missiles are all liquid fuel, and hence vulnerable to first strike attack. The few hundreds bombs can only be delivered by ageing Soviet-designed bombers, which would have little chance of penetrating Soviet air defences. One submarine had been produced in 1970, with missile launch tubes, but the missiles were not tested until ten years later. Thus despite all the development effort, there seems to be little effort to make the force credible. It has been suggested[18] that China has not worried about fielding an invulnerable second strike force because it no longer believes that there is a threat from the Soviet Union: or that the people's war doctrine, with a limited nuclear capability, and credible civil defence is an adequate deterrent posture; or that it is worth waiting, despite the risk, until technology makes these weapons cheaper. The tests of the long range missile, CSS-4, in May 1980 show that the intention to keep up the development programme remains. That it is prepared to bear the economic burden, without gaining a significant operational capability, suggests that China's strategy is predominantly that of an insurance policy, against future world developments.

CHAPTER SEVEN

INDIAN NUCLEAR STRATEGY

India has a tradition of atomic energy research, which can rival that of the other nuclear powers. Homi J. Bhabha, the father of the Indian bomb, set up an institute of nuclear physics research in 1945. Three years later, the Indian Atomic Energy Commission was set up; but little was done until the formation of the Department of Atomic Energy in 1954. The first research reactor, APSARA, went critical in August 1956, and at the inauguration of the Atomic Energy Establishment the following January, Nehru said:

> ... *No man can prophesy the future. But I should like to say on behalf of my Government – and I think I can say with some assurance on behalf of any future Government of India – that whatever might happen, whatever the circumstances, we shall never use this atomic energy for evil purposes.*[1]

Under Nehru a joint Canada-India reactor, CIRUS, was set up and became operational in 1960. With a second research reactor in 1961 and a plutonium plant completed in 1964, the Indians had a sound base for nuclear weapon production. Nehru's commitment for future governments was somewhat modified by his successor, Shastri. In November 1964, he told the Indian parliament that the policy was not rigid, but 'I have no doubt that we cannot at the moment think in terms of making atom bombs'.[2] The reasons were more likely to be economic than technical. Some observers[3] maintain that India could have produced an atom bomb before China, had it wished so to do.

INDIA AND PROLIFERATION

Indian public opinion was becoming more concerned about the dangers of a world divided into the nuclear 'haves' and 'have-nots'. The Sino-Indian conflict of 1962, the Chinese nuclear test in 1964, and the war with Pakistan in 1965 produced a strong body of opinion favouring nuclear weapons for India.[4] Just a week after the first Chinese test, the revered Bhabha broadcast on the subject of disarmament. He maintained that the United Nations would need a security force, armed with nuclear weapons, to police a disarmed world. He made the point that 'One must remember that it is not any object which is intrinsically good or bad, but the use which is made of it'.[5] He went on to explain that the attraction of atomic explosions for peaceful engineering purposes meant that the rapid spread of nuclear weapons was likely.

India was a leading opponent of the Non-Proliferation Treaty (NPT), which was viewed as a discriminatory arrangement, set up by the nuclear weapon states for their own benefit. They identified three major areas of unfairness. Firstly, the 'haves' would be free to improve their nuclear arsenals, both in quantity and quality. The 'have-nots' would be prohibited from military research. Secondly, the nuclear weapon states did not have to submit to safeguards, while the others would have to submit even when engaging in peaceful nuclear activities. Thirdly, all transfers of any nuclear technology were subject to safeguards for the non-nuclear weapon states, while no transfers of the nuclear weapon states were affected.[6] The Indian representative at the NPT talks in 1967 remarked that the institution of such international controls was 'like an attempt to maintain law and order in a society by placing all its law-abiding citizens in custody, while leaving its law-breaking elements free to roam the streets'.[7]

THE PEACEFUL NUCLEAR EXPLOSION

Even after India finally rejected the NPT in 1967, there was no apparent urgency to complete the work on the atomic bomb. Indira Gandhi maintained that the option for Peaceful Nuclear Explosions (PNEs) was being retained. On 18 May 1974, an underground test explosion of a Hiroshima-sized device was successfully carried out. It was seen as a great boost to India's prestige. The stated purpose of the test was to continue research into PNEs, and the Indian literature of the time abounds with schemes for using PNEs in engineering projects, such as making harbours, hollowing out gas storage cavities, and extracting minerals and oil. All this despite the declining interest in America and Russia, and the emerging world scientific view that the disadvantages of nuclear explosives outweighed the advantages.[8]

There were other views as to the use of nuclear explosions. Writing just before the test, the Director of the Indian Institute of Defence Studies drew attention to the difference in treatment which Washington gave to India and China. Quoting one of President Nixon's aides as saying that 800 million Chinese armed with nuclear weapons could not be ignored, he speculated that 600 million Indians similarly armed might prompt a visit from a future American President to New Delhi.[9] Another commentator writing at the time of the test was rather more specific about the role of the PNE:

It cannot be denied that India's PNE has military implications as well. It demonstrates India's capabilities in the nuclear field and is a step in the direction of establishing India as a centre of independent decision-making in the world.[10]

The reason that the Gandhi government decided to carry out the test should give some indication of the Indian nuclear strategy. One commentator[11] cites three different reasons for the decision: to divert attention from the growing domestic problems; to force China to become more accommodating; and as a signal to the superpowers that India could not be taken for granted. The decision to conduct the test must have been taken in late 1970 or early 1971.[12] It is difficult to point to any one of the three suggested reasons as being of overwhelming significance at that time. Perhaps the decision was more an acquiescence to the requests of the scientists, given a feeling that there might be a measure of political kudos from a successful test.

Canada suspended all nuclear aid following the test explosion, and the United States took some mildly punitive action. Nevertheless, the Gandhi government kept the option of further tests open. No further tests were undertaken, and Prime Minister Desai has assumed a Nehru-like view of nuclear weapons while in office. The Indian External Affairs Minister stated at the United Nations on 30 September 1977 that, 'It is our solemn resolve that whatever the rest of the world may do, we will never use atomic energy for military purposes'.[13] The following year, Desai went further and said, 'We do not want to have any atomic weapons under any conditions, and do not want even to have explosions of any kind'.[14] Even if these statements were true, the return of Mrs Gandhi to power on 14 January 1980 made them of little relevance. Since taking office, she has accelerated India's military modernisation programme and a successful satellite launch has been carried out.[15] It would appear that the Gandhi government intends to keep open its nuclear option.

FUTURE TRENDS

If India had been stockpiling nuclear weapons, it could have produced some tens of weapons from the available plutonium. It has a limited delivery capability with its Canberra bomber force, and perhaps the recently acquired Jaguar aircraft. It is developing its satellite and missile technology, but would require a considerable investment of time and money to develop a force with the range and numbers necessary to pose a deterrent threat to China. While it could use its current potential nuclear force against Pakistan, it has no need to. Nevertheless, the concensus view is that India is continuing to keep the nuclear option open.[16] This suggests that it has opted for the 'insurance policy' approach to nuclear strategy. While denouncing nuclear weapons, India is prepared to devote hard-pressed resources to ensuring that it does not leave itself open to nuclear blackmail in the future.

CHAPTER EIGHT

ISRAELI NUCLEAR STRATEGY

The six countries examined previously have all demonstrated by the means of a test explosion their capability to produce atomic weapons. Israel has neither openly tested a nuclear device, nor claims to have a nuclear arsenal. Nevertheless, there is sufficient belief in the existence of an Israeli nuclear stockpile for it to have a credible nuclear deterrent strategy.

It has been said that Israel has always been a nuclear country.[1] Within a year of the establishment of the state in 1948, the first plans for the nuclear research programme had been made. The Israel Atomic Energy Commission was established in 1952 and was, significantly, placed within the Defence Ministry. No written terms of reference were produced for the Commission. Israeli scientists were sent abroad for training, an agreement was signed with France in 1953 for atomic cooperation, and another with the United States in 1954. A research reactor was purchased from the United States and became critical in 1960 at Nahal Soreq. This reactor was not a plutonium producer, and was unlikely to be used for weapon production purposes.

WEAPON PRODUCTION CAPABILITY

In 1957, Israel and France concluded a secret agreement which was to result in a large research reactor being built for the Defence Ministry at Dimona in the northern Negev. All the members of the Atomic Energy Commission resigned in 1957 and it has been suggested[2] that this was to indicate their opposition to the military uses of the proposed reactor. In late 1964, the Dimona reactor became critical, and started producing about 8kg of plutonium per year: enough for between one and two fission weapons after reprocessing.[3] It was suggested that the French-Israeli cooperation extended to the testing of a jointly designed atomic bomb at France's Sahara testing ground.[4] There have also been improbable reports of a secret underground test in the Negev in 1963.[5] Whether either of these reports is true does not effect the capability of Israel to produce nuclear weapons. Professor Van Cleave, looking at the need for tests, concluded:

> For 'first generation' fission bombs, testing by the Nth country would not be required for development ... By now, certainly, it can be confidently assumed that the basic design will work without testing, and work within a reasonable degree of predictability ... a test of a first-generation nuclear weapon by an Nth country has more political than technical significance.[6]

Having established a steady production system for plutonium fissile material, a reprocessing plant was necessary for rapid conversion to weapons' grade ore. The design of such a plant is distinctive, and there is thus agreement that Israel did not build one. The reason for this omission appears to be that Israel was successful in illegally acquiring a significant stock of enriched uranium. CIA reports have revealed that Israel obtained 'large quantities of enriched uranium by clandestine means'.[7] The New York Times report of this reminded readers of the loss of highly enriched uranium from the Nuclear Materials and Equipment Corporation in Apollo, Pennsylvania in 1965. Keeping track of nuclear fuel is always difficult; however, of the 382 pounds missing, the investigating commission decided that at least 206 pounds could not be accounted for as 'lost in the pipes'. This is sufficient for about 14 bombs.[8]

If Israel did manage to obtain nuclear weapon material in 1965, it would explain why no plutonium reprocessing plant was built. With an assured uranium capability, it could use the slower, but politically uncontroversial, method of 'hot laboratory' plutonium separation gradually to increase its stockpile.[9]

NUCLEAR POSTURE

Premier Eshkol in 1966, President Katzir in 1974 and Premier Rabin in 1975 have all stated that Israel will not be the first to introduce nuclear weapons into the Middle East.[10] This somewhat cryptic posture is useful in increasing the uncertainty of Israel's potential enemies. A report[11] in 1976 of a CIA briefing claimed that the Israeli arsenal of 13 weapons was prepared for possible use at the start of the 1973 war. Defence Minister Moshe Dyan was quoted in the report as justifying the Israeli nuclear option as, 'Israel has no choice, with our manpower we cannot physically go on acquiring more and more tanks and more and more planes'. The readiness to use their nuclear weapons to fight, if they are in danger of being defeated, indicates that the 'no first use' policy is rhetoric.

Israel's seriousness in obtaining a credible nuclear capability can also be seen in the procurement of suitable delivery systems. Nuclear warheads could be fitted to Jericho, Lance and Harpoon missiles; nuclear bombs could be dropped by F-4E Phantoms, Kfir-C2s, F-15s or even A-4 Skyhawks. Israel tried to purchase Pershing missiles from the United States in 1975, but withdrew the request when it provoked considerable controversy in Washington.[12] Certainly Jericho, Lance and, had it been procured, Pershing, make more military sense in a nuclear role than in a conventional one.

There is little doubt that Israel is a nuclear weapon state. Initially it raced, by all possible methods, to provide itself with a last resort capability. This could be used if there was an imminent danger of being 'pushed into the sea' by its Arab enemies. It may now be developing a nuclear war-fighting capability, to compensate for its numerical inferiority. Its ambiguous position does not appear to have deterred its opponents from aggression. One Israeli strategist has suggested, 'To maximise the odds of security and peace, Israel must adopt a doctrine of explicit strategic nuclear deterrence'.[13] An open declaration of nuclear capability might result in Soviet nuclear guarantees to the Arabs, or a reduction in support from the United States. Its strategy is therefore unlikely to change, and it will remain prepared to use nuclear weapons if the need arises.

CHAPTER NINE

DETERRENCE IN PRACTICE

The examination of the nuclear strategies of the seven nuclear weapon states shows that the reasons behind the acquiring of nuclear arsenals, and the practical objectives for their employment, vary not only from country to country but also from one time to another. Inevitably deterrence theory, as examined in the first part of this book, has tended to concentrate on the question of the design and utility of nuclear deterrence between the superpowers. Yet even between these two, theory and practice do not always seem to be in step. A number of factors seem to be important in the original decision to produce nuclear weapons. Certainly, in the cases examined, each country had a good scientific and technological base on which to carry out the development. Other countries with equivalent capabilities have not developed nuclear weapons, and it is useful to tabulate the factors which may have prompted the decision in the first seven to do so.

Table 1 gives a simplified breakdown of the objectives of each of the seven countries, as they emerge from this examination. World power status is, or was, of importance to the first five nuclear powers, who are also the permanent members of the United Nations Security Council. While the possession of nuclear weapons does confer such status, they are certainly now a requirement. National security objectives are common to all nuclear states. It appears that countries seeking ideological leadership in the world see a need to be nuclear armed. It might be possible to add India to this category, on the grounds that it was wishing to maintain the leadership of the

TABLE ONE

Comparison of National Reasons for Nuclear Arms

OBJECTIVE	UNITED STATES	USSR	BRITAIN	FRANCE	CHINA	INDIA	ISRAEL
World power status	Yes	Yes	Originally	Originally	Future plan	Possibly	—
National security	Yes	Yes	Yes	Yes	Yes	Originally	Yes
Ideological leadership	Yes	Yes	—	—	Yes	—	—
Local area leadership	—	Yes	—	Yes	Yes	—	—
Alliance obligations	Yes	Yes	Yes	Originally	—	—	—
Second decision centre	—	—	Yes	Yes	—	—	—
To offset conventional weaknesses	Yes	—	Yes	Yes	—	—	Yes
Internal prestige	—	—	Possibly	Yes	—	Yes	—
Insurance against future changes in alliances	—	—	Yes	Yes	—	Possibly	Possibly
Scientific or military pressures	Yes	Yes	Yes	Yes	—	Yes	Possibly
Reaction to possible nuclear threat	Yes Germany	Yes Germany and USA	Yes Germany and USSR	Yes USSR	Yes USA and USSR	Yes China	—
CURRENT POSTURE	Deterrence by matching the USSR arsenal	Deterrence by denial of victory	Second decision centre and insurance policy	Proportional deterrence and insurance policy	People's war with minimum deterrent	Insurance against future need	Deterrence by denial of victory

non-aligned states. However, as there is no evidence to support this, it has not been added. Only slightly different is the concept of local area leadership. France certainly looked upon nuclear weapons as a counter to German conventional dominance. Alliance obligations can be viewed as an extension of national security for those countries within alliances. The second decision centre or – more unkindly – the nuclear trigger, is a role for the lesser nuclear powers within alliances. It could in a somewhat different sense be applied to lesser nuclear powers, perhaps India and Israel, if they wished to be able to involve the superpowers and thus gain their assistance. Although Israel may have used this tactic to gain arms from the United States, it has not been included. The procurement of nuclear weapons to offset conventional weaknesses, or save on manpower, is a tendency among the Western countries. It can reduce the expense of keeping large standing conventional forces, justify expansion of nuclear arsenals, but inevitably turns into a nuclear war-fighting force. The development of nuclear weapons to generate internal prestige may be a factor. However, the long development time necessary means that it is unlikely to be the major objective; it may just affect the timing of the programme. As the practical use of nuclear weapons in the present world becomes more difficult to justify, the objective of keeping a deterrent force as an insurance policy against an unknown future is developing force as a justification. Britain and France openly hold this view, and India must be keeping its option open on these grounds. There seems to be evidence to suggest that scientific and military pressures underlie the decision to go nuclear in all cases – except possibly that of China. The weapons are scientifically interesting and militarily powerful. The combination tends to put pressure on the political decision makers to continue weapon development. Finally, as a variation on the general question of national security, the decision may be taken as a reaction to a perceived nuclear threat from another nation. Thus, initially, the Allies believed that Germany was well on the way to developing an atomic bomb. Although the table points to America as the threat perceived by the USSR, this may only be valid for the development of thermonuclear weapons.

The short summaries of current postures are designed to do

no more than indicate the differences between the nations. The postures and future trends that have been considered are relevant when the factors affecting future stability are examined in the final part of this book. It has been shown that the United States and the Soviet Union have large nuclear arsenals, and an ability to use nuclear weapons at all levels of conflict. Britain and France maintain small, but nevertheless effective, nuclear forces which will insure their security against the uncertain future. China has the potential for much greater development, but as yet, probably for economic reasons, remains a lesser nuclear power. India has in effect reverted to the position of a near nuclear weapon power. Only Israel appears to have both the capability and the likely need to use nuclear weapons, in a way which might ensure survival.

Part III

Future Stability

CHAPTER TEN

STABILITY AND AGREEMENTS

There is a widespread belief that the security of the world can be best improved by the negotiation of arms control agreements. These agreements are designed to reduce the risk of nuclear war, and should such a war start, make it easier to stop and less destructive. To determine what scope there is for improving stability through agreements, the achievements of the past will be examined, before considering lessons for the future.

Table 2 lists the major agreements that have been reached in the past 25 years, and which might have some influence on nuclear deterrence. For convenience they can be divided into four broad classes: restriction on location, restriction on weapon development, limitation on weapon numbers, and communication improvement measures. In addition, although not strictly an agreement, the question of unilateral acceptance of nuclear weapon restrictions is examined.

RESTRICTION ON LOCATION

The Antarctic and Seabed treaties proved attractive as no countries were intending to develop nuclear capabilities in these areas. They improved stability in as much as they removed possible areas of conflict, and reduced the area in which nuclear weapons could be deployed. It is unlikely that any other areas of mutual disinterest are to be found. The Outer Space Treaty has, by banning nuclear weapons from space, certainly

TABLE TWO

Major Agreements of the Past Twenty Five Years

Short Title	Agreed	In Force	No of Signatories	Provisions and Amendments
Antarctic Treaty	1959	1961	27	Prohibits all military activity and nuclear tests in the Antarctic.
Hot-line agreement	1963	1963	2	Establishes direct communication link between Washington and Moscow. Updated (1971). Similar links: UK-USSR (1967); France-USSR (1966).
Partial Test Ban Treaty	1963	1963	112	Prohibits nuclear tests in the atmosphere, outer space, or underwater. Further unratified treaties limit size of tests (1974) or PNEs (1976).
Outer Space Treaty	1967	1967	85	Prohibits nuclear weapons in Space, or military activity on celestial bodies.
Tlatelolco Treaty	1967	1968	23	Prohibits development, possession, testing or deployment of nuclear weapons by Latin American parties.
Non-Proliferation Treaty	1968	1970	121	Prohibits non-nuclear weapon states from acquiring nuclear weapons by manufacture or transfer of technology.
Sea-Bed Treaty	1971	1972	74	Prohibits nuclear weapons, and other weapons of mass destruction, on sea-bed beyond 12 mile national limits.
Nuclear Accidents Agreement	1971	1971	2	US-USSR agreement on measures to reduce the possibility of an outbreak of nuclear war by accident. Further agreement in 1973. Similar agreements: French-USSR (1976); UK-USSR (1977).
SALT I ABM Treaty	1972	1972	2	Limits US and USSR to two ABM sites each. 1974 protocol reduced limit to one site each.
SALT I Interim Agreement	1972	1972	2	Limits numbers of land-based and submarine based ICBMs held by US and USSR.
Biological Warfare Convention	1972	1975	99	Prohibits development, production or retention of biological weapons.
CSCE Helsinki Agreement	1975	1975	35	Includes agreement to pre-notify large scale military manoeuvres and exchange observers, with other confidence building measures.
ENMOD Convention	1977	1978	42	Prohibits military use of major environmental modification.
SALT II	1979	—	2	Limitations on numbers of launch vehicles, and MIRVs. Agreement to progress arms control measures. Unratified by USA.
Inhuman Weapons Convention	1981	—	23	Prohibits or restricts weapons which have excessively injurious or indiscriminate effects.

restrained expenditure in this field, and has probably reduced the chances of accidental nuclear contamination which could result from a technical failure. It has not halted research into various aspects of future warfare beyond the earth's atmosphere. Whatever the military advantages of an orbiting nuclear weapon system, the political drawbacks of the resulting increase in world tension makes such a development both unlikely and unattractive. The Tlatelolco Treaty was an attempt to create a nuclear weapon free zone in Latin America. While it may have had a marginal positive effect on stability by reducing the area available for the deployment of nuclear weapons, there is little evidence that it has reduced the interest shown by Argentina and Brazil in their nuclear weapon orientated research.

The most significant of the treaties which restrict the spread of nuclear weapons must be the Non-Proliferation Treaty (NPT). There is a widely held view that the danger of nuclear war increases significantly as the number of nuclear weapon states increases. It is therefore considered to be a desirable aim to prevent more nations from gaining a nuclear weapon capability. The argument is by no means self-evident. The only occasion on which nuclear weapons have been used in war was at a time when there was only one nuclear armed country. If bipolar deterrence has prevented war between the United States and the USSR, could not nuclear proliferation restrain other powers from war, and hence improve stability? General Beaufre, in making the case for the French deterrent, concludes that, 'The stability provided by the nuclear weapon is attainable only between reasonable power. Boxes of matches should not be given to children'.[1] On the other hand, Professor Waltz, in an examination of the problem of proliferation came to the optimistic conclusion that:

> *The measured and selective spread of nuclear weapons does not run against our interests and can increase the security of some states at a price they can afford to pay. It is not likely that nuclear weapons will spread with a speed that exceeds the ability of their new owners to adjust to them.*[2]

The fortunate lack of any history of nuclear conflicts makes it impossible to judge where the truth lies, as to what effect proliferation may have on future stability. It can, however, be said that proliferation has not been as rapid as was once expected. The seven nuclear nations examined in Part Two all had a significant background of advanced physics, chemistry and engineering research work to draw upon. They were run by stable forms of government, and had sufficient resources to devote to what they saw as an important national need. Measures taken against India, following its nuclear test, appear to have slowed further progress. Economic considerations have affected the development of nuclear weapons in several of the states. The NPT helped to slow the spread of nuclear weapons. Certainly a gradual spread, rather than a rapid increase, in the number of nuclear weapon states must be better for future stability. One detailed analysis by Cannizzo of the capabilities and strategic concerns of possible proliferation states sees the immediate problem as limited to perhaps as few as ten countries: Argentina, Brazil, India, Iran, Israel, Japan, Pakistan, South Africa, South Korea and Taiwan.[3] It has already been assumed in this study that two of these are nuclear weapon states. The remainder, although giving cause for concern, represent a more limited problem for the future than is sometimes suggested.

The major concerns about proliferation are often expressed as: governments which are more reckless in risk taking; governments which are unstable; a lack of weapon security; a greater number of decision makers within the nuclear release organisation of a small country; ambiguous command chains; first strike vulnerability; and irrational leaders. The extensive research programmes the considerable expense and the difficulties in obtaining the required materials make the development of nuclear weapons by unstable governments more difficult. The NPT and the control of nuclear technology and material slow the spread, and should therefore be continued. To improve security of weapons and reduce ambiguity of command, the technology for control of warheads (Permissive Action Links) should be made readily available to new nuclear weapon states. Although it can be argued that this would be condoning nuclear proliferation, the advantages in improving control of nuclear weapons outweigh these considerations. As a counter to the irrational leader or 'crazy state' acquiring a nuclear capability, such pre-emptive actions as the Israeli attack on the Iraqi Osirak facility will need the tacit agreement of the superpowers.

If the NPT brings some benefit to future stability by slowing the spread of nuclear weapons, it has been suggested that the extension of the nuclear free zone concept might also bring restraining benefits. The European Nuclear Disarmament movement actively proposes that such a zone should be established in Europe.[4] The British Government view is that, 'Talk of a European nuclear free zone is one sided and naive. It ignores the realities of Soviet military power; it ignores the facts of geography'.[5] Certainly, as was discussed in Part One, the presence of tactical nuclear weapons in the path of any Soviet invasion increases the credibility of their use and hence enhances deterrence. On the other hand, one strategic analyst, Professor Richard Garwin, while being no disarmer considers that the liabilities of tactical weapons outweigh the benefits.[6] He cites the dangers of accidental or unauthorised use by local commanders, capture by the enemy or the host country, theft, terrorism and also the significant manpower requirement for maintenance and guarding. He proposes replacing tactical nuclear weapons by a system of shared targeting and release of a portion of the United States based missile force, which now have the accuracy, range and flexibility to be used in this role. While logically the control would be no different from the present dual key arrangement, it is unlikely that this arrangement would appeal to either the American or European politicians. In theory, credibility ought not to be altered, but the change could be perceived as a reduction in commitment to Europe by America. Control of escalation, should deterrence fail, would be made easier.

Whether or not a scheme for a nuclear weapon free Europe were adopted, there is little prospect of preventing nuclear weapons from being targeted on Europe in an all out war. In the event of a strategic nuclear exchange between the United States and the USSR, both geography and strategy point to the likelihood of the devastation of Europe. A nuclear free zone might reduce the credibility of the deterrent, while not reducing the dangers should deterrence fail. It is, therefore, not a proposal which would improve the stability of the world for the future.

WEAPON DEVELOPMENT RESTRICTIONS

Restrictions on weapon development have taken the form of either restrictions on testing, or the restriction of particular types of weapon. In either case the motivation for the agreement has been mutual self interest of the signatories. The partial test ban treaty reduced the world health risk from nuclear tests and made proliferation more difficult, while not hampering the continued development of nuclear weapons. It is argued by some that a Comprehensive Test Ban (CTB) is of vital importance to future stability. Lord Zuckerman wrote:

Talk of a balanced reduction of forces – to which all sides are committed – will remain mere words until a presumptive CTB is successfully negotiated.[7]

While this may be an unnecessarily pessimistic view, there is no doubt that the moral position of the nuclear weapon states, with regard to the NPT, is open to criticism as long as they continue to test new warheads, albeit underground. On balance the prohibition, either complete or partial, of nuclear weapon testing by agreement is unlikely to have a significant effect on the future stability. France and China have both demonstrated that the moral pressures to conform to such agreements is insufficient when they feel matters of national security are at risk.

The prohibition of weapons of particular kinds is not a new concept, and the 1972 agreement on bacteriological weapons was in accord with the tradition of banning weapons which seemed unnecessarily frightful. Although not strictly relevant to the question of nuclear weapons and future stability, the difficulties in verification of such prohibitions are directly applicable to attempts to ban particular nuclear weapons (or indeed all nuclear weapons). The most interesting restriction on weapon types was the Anti-Ballistic Missile (ABM) treaty concluded as part of the first Strategic Arms Limitations Talks (SALT). It has been claimed that the treaty demonstrates that both the United States and the USSR accept that stability comes from mutual deterrence.

By the time the SALT talks began in Helsinki in late 1969, they were agreed on the existence of and the need to preserve parity, mutual deterrence and strategic stability.[8]

The alternative explanation for the agreement was that it was a rational economic measure, designed to prevent an unproductive arms race, in which each development in the defence could be countered at less cost by the offence. It can be argued that, by permitting the deployment of a limited ABM system and by allowing research and development to continue, the treaty did little to enhance the prospects for future stability.

Both superpowers are currently showing considerable interest in developing new ABM technology. The High Frontier study[9] in the United States advocates a comprehensive layered space-based missile defensive system, which it claims is practical, affordable and desirable. The practicality has yet to be demonstrated. The directed energy (lasers or particle beams) or kinetic energy kill systems suggested have yet to prove that they are even technically feasible for the task of destroying missiles in their early booster phase. Even if the technical problems, and in some cases the laws of physics, could be overcome given sufficient money, 'leakage' would still occur. A totally effective defence against ballistic missiles is not in prospect. Given that, the enemy can counter by deploying a larger number of offensive missiles, at significantly less cost. Working at the limits of current technology is inevitably expensive; and space-based systems themselves are extremely vulnerable, which means that the expense would be multiplied by the number of redundant systems which would need to be deployed. Finally, were it possible to deploy an effective protective system, the effect on strategic stability is arguable. Certainly it is sensible for both superpowers to continue research into developing effective counters to any defensive system that the other might deploy. Such research reduces the incentive for either side to abrogate the ABM Treaty. This has one other effect. The restriction on ABM system deployment has made the United States and the Soviet Union more vulnerable to the lesser nuclear powers. In as much as multiple decision centres improve deterrence, as discussed previously, the ABM Treaty improves the prospects for future stability.

If the current nuclear weapons are adequate to provide nuclear deterrence and stability, it can be argued that the development of new types can only be counter-productive. In this case, a prohibition on development of any new weapon system would have both strategic and economic merit. It is by such a simple analysis that the advocates of a 'nuclear freeze' make their case. A comprehensive freeze proposal would require a ban on all further production, testing or deployment of nuclear weapons and their delivery systems.[10] Such an omnibus agreement would meet with impossible difficulties when it came to detailed negotiations. For example, the development of civilian satellite launching capabilities could be used to improve missile capabilities. It would be impossible to isolate industrial research from many kinds of military research. Dual-capable aircraft could rapidly be converted to nuclear role. Cruise missiles are particularly easy to develop covertly. The most difficult of all, the possibility of covert production of weapons' grade material would have to be covered. This already is a difficult problem in the NPT context. Overall, the problems of verification appear insurmountable. For all these reasons, such a scheme designed to stop the inexorable march of military technology must be as unlikely to succeed in the present world as general and complete disarmament.

LIMITATIONS ON WEAPON NUMBERS

The major success in limiting the overall number of nuclear weapon launching systems was achieved by SALT I. Although the number of missiles of various categories was frozen, modernisation was permitted, and no restrictions were placed on the number of warheads on each missile. An agreement which in effect recognises the futility of an ever increasing strategic nuclear arsenal may improve the prospects for peace; it does not necessarily improve the prospects for future stability. Raymond Garthoff has identified the resulting tendency to develop weapons not covered by limitations agreements, to be used as 'bargaining chips' at the next round of talks.[11] He cites the Cruise missile, for which there was no strategic need in 1972, as a prime example. Thus restrictions on weapons numbers in a particularly category can lead to a proliferation of new weapon types, which is unlikely to improve stability. He saw the failure to prohibit multiple warheads as a major failure of SALT I, as this enabled each side to increase its number of deliverable warheads, and hence increase the incentives for striking first.[12]

There is no doubt that arms limitation agreements become progressively more difficult to negotiate as, inevitably, those areas which are non-controversial, verifiable and acceptable to domestic public opinion are dealt with first. The prolonged process of SALT II, with its subsequent lack of ratification by the American Congress, and the endless talks in Vienna on mutual and balanced force reductions, show the difficulties of further limitations. As one commentator, Blechman, said: 'The implicit promise was that the arms control process would continue, and that each stage would have more ambitious goals'.[13] In the event the partial test ban has not become a complete one; the Antarctic, Seabed and Outer Space treaties have not extended into other areas; and SALT I did not lead to significant constraints on numbers of nuclear warheads. It is arguable as to whether their mutual suspicion and mistrust was increased. Paul Nitze, who was a member of the American delegation from 1969 to 1974, is in no doubt that, 'The merits of SALT II were almost entirely illusory'.[14] George Ignatieff, Canadian Ambassador to the Geneva disarmament conference said, 'Bringing the nuclear capabilities of the superpowers down to a minimum necessary to deter war is a reasonable objective, but one which has certainly not been brought any closer to realisation by SALT'.[15] The experiences of the Strategic Arms Reduction Talks, and the Intermediate Range Nuclear Force talks in 1982 and 1983 illustrated the difficulty in achieving even specialised agreements when the relations between negotiating states were poor. Arms control is declared to be a policy objective by most nuclear powers. It has had remarkably little success in the past and is unlikely to be a major factor in future stability.

COMMUNICATION IMPROVEMENT MEASURES

There has, rightly, been considerable concern lest a nuclear war be started by accident or miscalculation. Measures which improve the communications between the nuclear powers must help to reduce this possibility, and also offer opportunities to terminate a war if it should start. It was such an appreciation after the Cuban missile crisis, which led to the memorandum of understanding for the installation of the Washington-Moscow 'hot-line'. The succeeding agreements to improve the quality of the line, and also its reliability, are an indication of the importance attached to it. Although its usefulness in times of crisis is unquestioned, its survivability in war is more suspect:

The satellite link is probably more secure and reliable than cable from the point of view of accidental interruption, but it is probably also more vulnerable to disruption in the event of any nuclear exchange – the very situation in which it would be most desperately needed.[16]

The link is essential in times of crisis to ensure that threats are not misunderstood; it is essential in times of peace to ensure that accidents do not happen. The preservation of the link in war, as a method of controlling hostilities, can only be assured by measures which are considered later.

As well as technical improvements to communications, efforts have been made to improve communications of intentions through Confidence Building Measures (CBMs). These aim to reduce tension by making military intentions explicit. The Conference on Security and Cooperation in Europe (CSCE) at Helsinki in 1975 agreed on prior notification of major military exercises, and the exchange of observers at such exercises. Such measures may 'help separate the unambiguous signals of hostile intent from the random noise of continuous military activity',[17] but are non-binding, and have little influence on nuclear military activities. Nevertheless, in as much as they can reduce international tension, at no political cost, and do not impair deterrence, their negotiation must be a reasonable aim. It is too early to say what contribution the Conference on Disarmament in Europe, currently taking place in Stockholm, will make to this process.

UNILATERAL NUCLEAR DISARMAMENT

The final path to stability through agreement to be considered here is that of total or partial disarmament. The goal of General and Complete Disarmament is a Utopian dream. As Professor Laurence Martin speaking in the 1981 Reith Lectures said:

> *Serious studies make it clear that General and Complete Disarmament demands world government, and even that would merely transform the problem into one of preventing civil war within the new state.*[18]

Morally laudable as it is, it is not a practical path for the foreseeable future.

If worldwide disarmament is unlikely, what of the option of any country unilaterally to disarm, either completely or in part? It can be claimed that continued modernisation of armaments increases international tension, and feeds an 'arms race', which continues spiralling upwards. A moral case for nuclear disarmament is often made:

> *Nuclear weapons explode the theory of just war ... our familiar notions about jus in bello require us to condemn even the threat to use them ... Nuclear war is and will remain morally unacceptable.*[19]

The mixture of the arms race view, and the moral argument, with a disbelief in the reality of the threat from the Soviet Union has led to a resurgence of the unilateral nuclear disarmament movement in Europe. While some European countries may reject 'dual key' nuclear weapons from their territory, it is only in Britain that the prospect of a country voluntarily dismantling its nuclear capability is a possibility.

To examine the effect on the future stability of the world of unilateral nuclear disarmament by Britain requires some assumptions on the resulting defence and foreign policies. Various possible alternative defence strategies are aired from time to time. They range from continuing all commitments unchanged, save for the lack of British nuclear weapons, through to a withdrawal from NATO, and relying on 'the military training of virtually the whole adult population and their organisation in non-professional militias in preparation for resistance in depth in the event of invasion'.[20] One much canvassed alternative defence policy would retain conventional forces, exclude American bases from Britain, and bring home troops stationed on the European mainland. Membership of NATO is not considered to be necessarily incompatible with this posture:

> *Although Britain would have established some distance from NATO strategy, it would still be desirable to exercise some influence in NATO, supporting for example, future positions of the Dutch Government similar to the one it now has about long-range theatre nuclear forces, supporting Danish and Norwegian interest in a Nordic nuclear-free zone against American objections.*[21]

Thus continued association with NATO is seen as a way of helping other members to break away from American influence. It seems highly probably that, were Britain to follow such a strategy, it would lead to the break up of NATO.

Although France detached itself from the military organisation though not the political aspects of the NATO Alliance, it did so while demonstrating increasing rather than decreasing nuclear strength. There is no doubt that unilateral disarmament by Britain would be viewed by allies and enemies alike as an indication of economic, political and moral weakness. A Europe that was experiencing the break up of NATO, a Britain that was perceived as lacking the will to defend itself, and an America sufficiently disillusioned to become isolationist is hardly a combination which would be conducive to world security. For this reason, any move towards unilateral disarmament by Britain is potentially destabilising.

CHAPTER ELEVEN

STABILITY AND TECHNOLOGY

It has been seen in Part Two how technological pressures were involved in the development of nuclear weapons. It is a widely held view that these technological development pressures are inherently bad and potentially destabilising. A former Chief Scientific Adviser, Lord Zuckerman, holds this view strongly:

> *It will take years before the great powers start living in peace. They never will unless several other things happen first. Above all, the nuclear threat must be reduced, and for that to come about the goal should be a halt to all R and D designed to elaborate new nuclear warheads and new means of delivery.*[1]

Given the concern expressed by many scientists over the future of world security, it is surprising that they do not carry out more research into those technologies which could improve stability. All too often, their efforts appear to be devoted to destructive criticism of all military research. Having examined the potentially destabilising technological advances, areas of research which might improve the prospects for peace will be suggested.

DESTABILISING TECHNOLOGY

Throughout the discussion of deterrence in Part One, the concept of the invulnerable second strike retaliatory force remained the bedrock upon which the other shifting strategies were placed. It is therefore probable that any technological development which renders this retaliatory capability less credible could have an adverse effect on future stability. This research can either be directed at the destruction of an enemy's nuclear force before it is launched, or at providing an assured defensive capability, which could prevent enemy warheads arriving at their targets.

The continuing improvements to missile systems has led to concern that one side or the other may believe that it can carry out a disarming first strike attack. The introduction of multiple independently-targetable re-entry vehicle technology has improved accuracy and increased the number of warheads on each missile. However, the higher accuracies achieved through satellite-based navigation systems and the computer terrain matching techniques of the Cruise missile make further enhancements of little significance in terms of stability. The silo-based missiles are now rather more at risk than they were in the past. The air-launched nuclear retaliatory forces remain as vulnerable as ever when on the ground. This leaves the submarine-based systems as the most fruitful, and hence potentially destabilising, area for counter-warfare research.

Anti-submarine warfare capability has undoubtedly been steadily improving. Increasing numbers of submarines coupled with increasing detection ranges, faster and more accurate identification and localisation techniques, and longer range weapons with higher kill probabilities have resulted in 'an anti-submarine force able to conduct increasingly rapid and effective operations within an expanding three dimensional undersea zone'.[2] However, incremental advances, or even some unexpected technological breakthrough, do not foreshadow the achievement of a pre-emptive capability against nuclear missile submarines. The US Commission on Strategic Forces agreed that:

The problem of conducting open-ocean search for submarines is likely to continue to be sufficiently difficult that ballistic missile submarine forces will have a high degree of survivability for a long time.[3]

Given the difficulties of coordination of strikes against all three basing systems of the nuclear forces of the United States and the Soviet Union, concern over the possibility of technology providing a first strike capability appears misplaced.

The other area for research is towards providing the assured defensive capability. A radical discovery which gave total assurance that all incoming warheads would be prevented from reaching their targets would probably have an adverse effect on stability. All defensive systems can achieve is a reduction in the probability that the incoming warheads will get through. As already discussed in the previous chapters, there is little prospect of a novel defensive system providing the assurance of safety which would be necessary to eliminate the deterring effect of nuclear weapons. Given the vast numbers of warheads available, and the relatively few nuclear strikes required to generate unacceptable damage by any criteria, development work on defensive systems is unlikely to have a critical effect on future stability.

STABILISING TECHNOLOGY

If the prospective technological developments are unlikely to reduce the deterrent power of nuclear weapons, can technology be directed towards areas where it might improve the prospects of future stability? It is not enough merely to suggest areas which may be good in an idealistic sense, but there must be obvious benefits to the states which pursue the development. As has already been discussed, it is in the interest of all parties to a potential nuclear conflict to be able to communicate with each other. It is also important that the nuclear weapon release authority be retained at the highest possible level, while not unduly hampering the response to any threat. These measures reinforce deterrence by allowing clear signals of intention to defend vital interests, and they also reduce the risk of war by accident or miscalculation. Should deterrence fail, the ability to control the subsequent escalation will make the deterrent threat more credible.

Should the United States or the Soviet Union believe that it is about to suffer a pre-emptive nuclear strike from the other, it currently has a number of response options available. The options divide into two categories: those which commit the states to unavoidable nuclear war – launch on warning, or launch on assessment; and those which give a good chance to retrieve the situation if some miscalculation has been made – launch of aircraft-based strike forces on recallable missions, or wait to ride out possible attack. Prudence would make the retrievable options more attractive, but by their nature they make the deterrent posture less effective, as they put at risk a proportion of the retaliatory force. The dilemma results from the present inability to recall missiles in the way that aircraft can be recalled to base. There is probably no reason why, given sufficient time and money, a missile which was literally recallable should not be developed. However, a much simpler and cheaper method of exercising control over a missile which has already been launched is to provide it with an arming and disarming mechanism which can be operated by radio signal.

Research should be directed towards providing all missiles with a facility for three possible operating modes: *safe*, *armed but can be disarmed in flight*, and *armed and locked*. The *safe* missile would equate to the normal missile configuration today, and require two men to bring it to the second mode and launch it. Once launched it would remain armed and targeted unless it received an appropriate coded signal from the leadership's command and control centre, via the satellite system which also carries the Hot Line. This would increase the incentive of either side to refrain from attacking these vital facilities, and hence make the control of a war, should it happen, more probable. In addition it would give a disincentive to both anti-ballistic missile measures and communication jamming, for fear of preventing the disarming signal getting through to the incoming missile. A fortuitous by-product of this system is the ability to render an accidentally launched missile inoperative; and thus end one of the major areas of concern for the start of a war by mistake. To reinforce this aspect, it would be useful to select automatically a target in an unpopulated area, or the sea, when the disarming of the warhead occurs.

There are a number of possible objections to this proposal. It may be argued that the enemy might find a way to activate the disarming mechanism; for this reason the third option of *armed and locked* would be available if necessary. Given the state of computer-based cypher techniques, it is unlikely that the coded disarming signal could be reproduced by the enemy. Scenario writers will object that one side could be duped into launching a large proportion of its missile force, which would subsequently be rendered useless by a rapid conciliatory move. This is an extremely improbable scenario, given the risks if any missiles fail to disarm, and the numbers of weapons which can be held in reserve. Finally, it will be suggested that such a system cannot be foolproof, and some missiles would not be disarmed before impact. This is undoubtedly true, but the advantages of research into an area which offers some prospect of an improvement in stability must outweigh this. The system offers an extra safeguard against accidental war, an incentive to preserve the leadership and the means of communication for negotiation and an improvement in the credibility of deterrence.

Currently, technology is directed towards improving the abilities of each side to wage war if deterrence should fail. The enhanced radiation weapon is one example. While such innovations may appear to make nuclear war-fighting marginally more credible, and hence enhance deterrence, it is unlikely that they will play any critical role in future stability. By suggesting one new area for research, it has been intended to show that technology could be directed towards both improving deterrence and stability.

One other area of technological development merits closer examination. Can technological developments of non-nuclear weapon systems improve the prospects for stability? The Steering Group of the European Security Study looked at possible ways of capitalising on new technologies in order to reduce NATO's need for the early use of nuclear weapons.[4] If developments in conventional weapons could offer the same deterrent effects as nuclear weapons, and at the same time delay the need for a nuclear decision, this could enhance deterrence through making it more credible, and could improve the possibility of controlling war should deterrence fail. The current proposals, however, do not appear to offer that assurance. The new technologies are very expensive and would in practice cause reductions in other military equipment programmes. The effect on the nuclear threshold is by no means obvious. One example of these proposals is the possibility of using some 600 Pershing II missiles, with conventional anti-airfield munition warheads, in order to attack 30 Warsaw Pact airfields.[5] The effect of the launch of such a massive ballistic missile attack, albeit conventional, on the nuclear threshold is debatable. Certainly the arms control implications are unhelpful. Technology must be used to improve conventional weapon capability, but it cannot offer the prospect of replacing a dependence on nuclear weapons. This is considered further in the following chapter on stability and strategy.

CHAPTER TWELVE

STABILITY AND STRATEGY

The studies in the first parts of this book have shown how widely the nuclear strategy can vary both over a period of time and from country to country. Yet the system has been stable: there has been no nuclear war. While concern has been expressed about particular strategies leading to instability, there has been remarkably little evidence to support such a view. The Cuban missile crisis of 1962 is normally considered the only occasion on which nuclear war has appeared likely. On this occasion, as was shown in Chapter 2, the power of nuclear deterrence was such as to make both leaders act very carefully. Forces were placed on alert during the 1973 Arab-Israeli conflict, but this appears to have been more as a forceful deterrent signal rather than any intention to start a nuclear war[1]. As Paul Bracken has pointed out:

Some people consider it remarkable that no nuclear weapons have been fired since 1945. Far more remarkable is the absence of a full Soviet-American alert. No American bombers have been launched in anticipation of enemy attack, at no time have nuclear weapons in Europe been dispersed from their peacetime storage sites, nor have all of the Soviet nuclear submarines been despatched from their ports at one time. Instead of the Munich world of blackmail backed by nuclear alerts that was predicted, we have had more than 35 years in which nuclear forces have been handled with kid-gloves, because national leaders have understood the dangers.[2]

The development of the strategy of flexible response has improved stability, in as much as it has reinforced the fears of the Soviets of the inevitability of American involvement following any expansion into Western Europe. It has been counter-productive in its self-deterring effect on the people of Western Europe. The alternative strategy of removing nuclear weapons from Europe and improving conventional forces was explained earlier. The proposal that such a move would improve deterrence by raising the nuclear threshold and thus improve credibility is unproven. Conventional forces have a poor record for deterring adventurism; chivalrous conventional response to conventional forces is by no means assured; and once the conventional forces of one side or the other face defeat, the decision to concede or to go nuclear needs to be made. For these reasons, and also the added expense of such a posture, a nuclear free Europe is not a useful alternative strategy to improve the prospects for future stability.

A strategy which explicitly declared that NATO would not be the first side to employ nuclear weapons, although not a novel proposal, has gained considerable support since it was advocated by four distinguished Americans in early 1982.[3] Such a policy, it is argued, would enhance deterrence by reassuring the Europeans that they would not be a nuclear battlefield for the superpowers, and at the same time reducing the risk to the United States of being dragged into a strategic nuclear exchange as a result of a European war. The adoption of such a policy would also force NATO nations into improving their conventional forces. Reducing the risk of nuclear escalation should stiffen the political will of NATO nations and hence improve deterrence. In reality, there are two possible outcomes of such a declaration by NATO: either the Warsaw Pact would believe the declaration, or it would not. In the first case deterrence would revert to an evaluation of the conventional balance: a prospect which historically is not one which can engender a great deal of confidence. In the second and more likely case, where the no first use declaration is not believed, then deterrence is not affected, although the particular force structures might be. It would appear to be unwise to make such a declaration in case it was believed. Changes in force structure should be analysed on their overall effect on deterrence.

Any proposed changes in strategy must be directed towards maintaining deterrence. Only if there is little risk that a new strategy may make the failure of deterrence more likely should it be adopted on the grounds that it will improve the outcome should deterrence fail. Many of the current arguments work from the reverse viewpoint: that the outcome, should deterrence fail, must be the least appalling; and that if the strategy makes that failure more likely, then that is unfortunate.

The risk of total devastation through nuclear war is the frightful prospect which deters. To ensure that governments realise that they do run this risk, the strategy must be such as to make recourse to nuclear weapons in any major conflict appear highly probable. Flexible response achieves this, but so did the previous tripwire strategy. Indeed, it has been suggested that there is little difference between the two, given the reluctance of Western nations to fund large conventional forces.[4] There are, however, some aspects of the force structure, which are so lacking in credibility that they add little to deterrence. In particular, battlefield nuclear weapons are unlikely to be usable. The time taken to obtain nuclear release, the political considerations in using such weapons in the crowded Central Region, the nature of their targets, and the vulnerability of the forces equipped with them, make them of little military value. If they have no effect on deterrence, do they influence the outcome if deterrence fails? They make the pressures on decision-makers stronger to take an early nuclear decision for fear that the weapons may be lost, and they invite the early use of nuclear weapons on themselves by the enemy. Once nuclear release has been authorised, these short range weapons are impossible to control effectively at the highest level. For all these reasons, the short range battlefield nuclear weapons are likely to make the outcome, should deterrence fail, worse rather than better, while their existence does not add to the overall deterrent posture. For this reason they should be withdrawn, with whatever arms control bonuses can be negotiated. The NATO decision in 1979 to reduce its stockpile of such weapons initially by 1000, and the subsequent 1983 decision to withdraw a further 1400[5] is a welcome indication that this view is gaining ground – in the West at least. Dual capable aircraft and artillery, which can use either conventional or nuclear weapons, are an area for detailed consideration. The introduction of the longer range nuclear missile systems (Cruise and Pershing II) may allow a more effective deployment of forces. Current dual-capable systems pose the commander with the dilemma as to what level of attrition to accept during a conventional phase of any conflict. Reverting to a wholly conventional role, in effect, generates extra conventional forces for no cost.

Another option for change is the adoption of a more automatic form of nuclear response to attack. Deterrence would be enhanced by demonstrating that any nuclear attack would inevitably bring a nuclear response. Such proposed 'launch on warning' systems would undoubtedly reduce concerns about the possibilities of successful pre-emptive attacks, but the drawbacks outweigh such considerations. The need for pre-delegated authority, and the risk of misassessment, would increase the dangers on unintentional nuclear war enormously. As pre-emptive attack is not a sensible option to either side, and the dangers of automatic response are so great, it is not in the interests of stability to move towards such a policy.

Finally, having considered possible changes to the overall declaratory nuclear strategy, one aspect of the detail of nuclear target planning policy should be considered. The ability to spare the leadership in order to negotiate must be built in at the target planning stage. From a purely military point of view, it is natural that the centres of command, both political and military, will feature high on target lists. Whatever the real target lists, the leadership of each side will anticipate that they are potential targets, and hence deterrence is not affected by an option to exclude control centres. Should deterrence fail, it is less likely that the war can be controlled or halted if the leadership and communication facilities have been destroyed. It would therefore be sensible for each side to base its strategy on an intention to preserve the enemy leadership and lines of communication during the early stages of a war.

CHAPTER THIRTEEN

PEACE AND THE REAL WORLD

As long as there are nuclear weapons in the world, there must be a strategic parity of nuclear forces so that neither side will venture to embark on a limited or regional nuclear war. Genuine security is possible only when based on a stabilization of international relations, a repudiation of expansionist policies, the strengthening of international trust, openness and pluralization in the Socialist societies, the observance of human rights throughout the world, the rapprochement – convergence – of the socialist and capitalist systems, and worldwide coordinated efforts to solve global problems.[1]

ANDREI SAKHAROV, 1983[1]

This book attempts to draw together the theories of the strategists, with the practices of the nuclear nations, and hence examine the prospect for future stability in the world.

The complex variations of deterrence theory, with their unreal assumptions of the predictability of decision makers under stress and with their imaginative scenarios, provided little more than a few basic common sense principles. The first principle is that nuclear weapons are sufficiently frightening to induce great caution among the decision makers, in circumstances where their use becomes remotely possible. To exercise nuclear deterrence, therefore, a country must show that it has a nuclear weapon capability and might be prepared to use it if its vital interests were threatened. These vital interests must be explained unambiguously, if deterrence is to operate.

The examination of national nuclear strategies showed that

there are wide variations in what each state considers is necessary for its nuclear stockpile. There may be some minimum size below which a pre-emptive strike by an enemy would remove all chances of nuclear retaliation. The evidence does not suggest that this minimum size is very large. At the other extreme, there is no evidence to suggest that large nuclear arsenals make the outbreak of war more likely. In general, it appears that nuclear deterrence is remarkably independent of the size and composition of the nuclear forces. In this respect, nuclear weapons differ significantly from conventional arms.

The examination of the factors affecting future stability gave little hope for the prospects of useful arms control agreements. While this may be regrettable from an economic and humanitarian aspect, the robustness of nuclear deterrence means that lack of arms control is unlikely adversely to affect world peace. That nuclear weapons are unlikely to be used does not make it any less important to attempt to improve the prospects for security. In particular, the control of nuclear weapons at the highest level and the security of the leadership and its communications must enhance the prospects both for deterrence, and for controlling conflict if deterrence should fail.

Nuclear weapons have reduced the risk of war between the nuclear states and have been a source of caution in the conduct of international relations. Fears that nuclear war is becoming ever more likely are based on extreme scenarios of first strike vulnerability, and also the fear of the probability of war by accident increasing with time. The conduct of governments, and the reality of the destructive power of nuclear weapons, make first strike scenarios illogical. The safety record of nuclear weapons, and their associated security measures which have been added to over the years, suggest that accidental war may be becoming less, rather than more, probable.

Nuclear weapons cannot be legislated or wished away. The use of modern nuclear systems on any scale would be a disaster beyond all experience. No military defence against such weapons is in prospect. Uncomfortable as it may be, nuclear deterrence offers the only prospect for preventing the use of nuclear weapons in the future. Deterrence can last as long as is necessary, and none of the alternatives can offer as stable a prospect.

It is always tempting to finish with a description of the writer's ideal world, in which neither war nor weapons are necessary. The mechanism for achieving such a state is left suitably vague, with a reference to the concerted efforts of all reasonable men. The real world does not work that way. Practical efforts to improve the prospect for peace in the future depend on the implementation of small changes, none of which cause large disturbances to the current power structures. Technology has a part to play in this, but it cannot provide the instant total solution. The utility of nuclear weapons lies in providing the backdrop of stable international relations, which may allow the time for any future age of peace and understanding to develop.

NOTES AND REFERENCES

INTRODUCTION

1 H. Schuch in W. Oldeberg, *Nobel the Man and His Prizes* (New York, 1972) p. 528.
2. Quoted in W. Wells, 'Our Technological Dilemma', *Bulletin of Atomic Scientists*, 16, November 1960, p. 363.

PART I

Nuclear Deterrence In Theory

1 THE THINKING MAN'S BOMB

1 B. Brodie, *The Absolute Weapon: Atomic Power and World Order* (Princeton: Arno, 1946) p. 76.
2 B. Brodie, *Strategy in the Missile Age* (Princeton University Press, 1959) p. 158.
3 Office of Technology Assessment, *The Effects of Nuclear War* (London: Croom Helm, 1980) p. 10.
4 Ibid., p. 8.
5 C. Sagan, 'Nuclear War and Climatic Catastrophe', *Foreign Affairs*, Winter 1983-4, p. 292.
6 A. Beaufre, *Deterrence and Strategy* (London: Faber & Faber, 1965) p. 36.
7 H. Kahn, *On Thermonuclear War*, 2nd edition (Princeton: Oxford University Press, 1961) p. 185.
8 B. Brodie, *War and Politics* (London: Macmillan Press, 1974) p. 64.
9 T. C. Schelling, *The Strategy of Conflict*, 2nd edition (London: Harvard University Press, 1980) pp. 260-61.
10 H. Kahn, *On Thermonuclear War*, op. cit., p. 96.
11 Henry Kissinger, *Nuclear Weapons and Foreign Policy* (London: Norton, 1957) pp. 135-36.

12 D. Ball, 'Can Nuclear War be Controlled?', *Adelphi Papers*, 169 (London: International Institute for Strategic Studies, 1981).

13 A. Beaufre, *Deterrence and Strategy*, op. cit., p. 55.

14 Henry Kissinger, *Nuclear Weapons and Foreign Policy*, op. cit., pp. 191-92.

15 G. Snyder, *Deterrence and Defense* (Princeton University Press, 1961) pp. 139-42.

16 R.L. Garwin in D.C. Gompert (ed.), *Nuclear Weapons and World Politics* (New York: McGraw Hill, 1977) pp. 104-8.

17 M. Carver, *A Policy for Peace* (London: Faber & Faber, 1982) pp. 106-7.

18 F. C. Iklé, 'NATO's First Nuclear Use: A Deepening Trap?', *Strategic Review*, Winter 1980, pp. 18-23.

19 K. Knorr and T. Read, *Limited Strategic War* (London: Pall Mall Press, 1962) p. 240.

20 G. Snyder, *Deterrence and Defense*, op. cit., p. 16.

21 R. Jervis, 'Deterrence Theory Revisited', *World Politics*, XXXII Jan 1979, p. 311.

22 H. Khan, *On Thermonuclear War*, op. cit., p. 185

23 A. L. George and R. Smoke, *Deterrence in American Foreign Policy* (New York: Columbia University Press, 1974) pp. 140-83.

24 K. N. Waltz, 'The Spread of Nuclear Weapons: More May Be Better', *Adelphi Papers* 171 (London: International Institute for Strategic Studies, 1981) pp. 19-20.

25 H. Kahn, *On Escalation* (New York: Pall Mall Press, 1965) pp. 57-58.

26 P. M. Morgan, *Deterrence: A Conceptual Analysis* (London: Sage Publications, 1977) p. 102.

27 B. Brodie, *Strategy in the Missile Age*, op. cit., p. 353.

28 B. Brodie, *War and Politics*, op. cit., p. 430.

PART II

National Strategy

2   UNITED STATES' NUCLEAR STRATEGY

1 D. A. Rosenberg, 'American Nuclear Strategy and the Hydrogen Bomb Decision', *Journal of American History*, 66, June 1979, p. 64.

2 B. Brodie, *The Absolute Weapon: Atomic Power and World Order* (Princeton: Arno, 1946) p. 73.

3 A. L. George and R. Smoke, *Deterrence in American Foreign Policy* (New York: Columbia University Press, 1974) pp. 134-36.

4 M. Mandelbaum, *The Nuclear Question* (Cambridge: Cambridge University Press, 1981) p. 47.
5 J. F. Dulles, 'Policy for Security and Peace', *Foreign Affairs*, 32, April 1954, p. 358.
6 G. W. Rathjens in F. Griffiths (ed.), *The Dangers of Nuclear War* (Toronto: University of Toronto Press, 1979) p. 136.
7 A. L. Friedberg, 'A History of US Strategic Doctrine – 1945 to 1980', *Journal of Strategic Studies*, 3, December 1980, pp. 40–41.
8 R. S. McNamara, 'Speech to American Bar Foundation, 17 February 1962', reproduced in J. Endicott & J. R. Stafford, *American Defense Policy* (London: Johns Hopkins University Press, 1977) p. 72.
9 R. S. McNamara, 'Speech at Ann Arbor, Michigan, 16 June 1962', reproduced in J. E. Endicott and J. R. Stafford, *American Defense Policy* (London: Johns Hopkins University Press, 1977) p. 74.
10 R. Kennedy, *13 Days* (London: Norton, 1969) p. 85.
11 A. L. George and R. Smoke, op. cit., p. 491.
12 R. S. McNamara, 'Statement before Committee on Armed Services, 24 February 1965', reproduced in J. E. Endicott and J. R. Stafford, *American Defense Policy* (London: Johns Hopkins University Press, 1977) p. 76.
13 R. S. McNamara, 'Statement before the House Armed Services Committee, FY 1968', reproduced in J.E. Endicott and J.R. Stafford, *American Defense Policy* (London: Johns Hopkins University Press, 1977) p. 39.
14 H. S. Rowen in L. Martin (ed.), *Strategic Thought in the Nuclear Age* (London: Heinemann, 1979) p. 148.
15 R. S. McNamara, 'Speech to Ann Arbor, Michigan, 16 June 1962', reproduced in J. E. Endicott and J. R. Stafford, *American Defense Policy* (London: Johns Hopkins University Press, 1977) pp. 74–75.
16 G. E. Miller in F. Griffiths (ed.), *The Dangers of Nuclear War* (Toronto: University of Toronto Press, 1979) p. 59.
17 R. M. Nixon, *US Foreign Policy for the 1970s, A Report to Congress, 18 February 1970*.
18 J. R. Schlesinger, *Annual Defense Department Report FY 1975*, Washington 1974, p. 36.
19 Ibid., p. 38.
20 D. M. Snow, *Nuclear Strategy in a Dynamic World* (Alabama: University of Alabama Press, 1981) p. 213.
21 D. H. Rumsfeld, *Annual Defense Department Report FY 1978*,

Washington 1977, pp. 67-68.
22 H. Brown, *Department of Defense Annual Report FY 1979*, Washington 1978, p. 33.
23 H. Brown, 'US Strategic Nuclear Policy Statement, 16 September 1980', Official Text from US Embassy dated 19 September 1980, p. 3.
24 *Strategic Survey 1980-1981* (London: International Institute for Strategic Studies, 1981) p. 12.
25 C. Weinberger, 'Testimony to the Senate Armed Forces Committee, 5 October 1981', *Survival*, XXIV January/February 1982, p. 29.
26 R. Reagan, 'Speech to the Nation, 23 March 1983', reprinted in *Survival*, XXV May/June 1983, p. 129.
27 B. Scowcroft, *President's Commission on Strategic Forces* (Washington: The Pentagon, 1983) p. 12.

3   SOVIET NUCLEAR POLICY

1 Statement by Igor N. Golovin in *The New York Times*, 19 August 1966.
2 Sir Anthony Eden, *Full Circle* (London: Cassell, 1960) p. 554.
3 N. S. Khrushchev, 'Khrushchev's Supreme Soviet Report on a Troop Cut, 15 January 1960', *The Current Digest of the Soviet Press*, XII 10 February 1960, p. 10.
4 H. Adomiet in J. Baylis and G. Segal (ed.), *Soviet Strategy* (London: Croom Helm, 1981) p. 191.
5 E. L. Warner, *The Military in Contemporary Soviet Politics* (New York: Praeger, 1977) p. 144.
6 R. L. Garthoff, 'SALT I: An Evaluation', *World Politics*, XXXI October 1978, p. 3.
7 J. D. Douglass and A. M. Hoeber, *Soviet Strategy for Nuclear War* (Stanford: Hoover Institute Press, 1979) p. 73.
8 Ibid., p. 16.
9 Ibid., p. 36.
10 G. Segal and J. Balyis (ed.), *Soviet Strategy*, op. cit., p. 22.
11 R. L. Arnett, 'Soviet Attitudes Towards Nuclear War: Do They Really Think They Can Win?', *The Journal of Strategic Studies*, 2, September 1979, pp. 182-83.
12 John Erickson, *Soviet Military Power* (London: Royal United Services Institute, 1971) pp. 7-8.
13 B. Crozier, *Strategy for Survival* (London: M. T. Smith, 1978) p. 76.
14 L. I. Brezhnev, 'Nuclear Weapons in Europe: A Soviet View', *Survival*, XXIV January/February 1982) p. 32.

15 Y. Andropov, Pravada Interview, translated in *Survival*, XXV May/June 1983, p. 131.
16 P. H. Nitze, 'Strategy in the Decade of the 1980s', *Foreign Affairs*, 59 Fall 1980.

4   BRITISH NUCLEAR STRATEGY

1 M. Gowing, *Independence and Deterrence*, Vol 1 (London: Macmillan Press, 1974).
2 Ibid., p. 169.
3 Ibid., p. 174.
4 L. Freedman, *Britain and Nuclear Weapons* (London: Macmillan Press, 1980) pp. 2-3.
5 R. N. Rosecrance, *Defence of the Realm* (New York: Columbia University Press, 1968) pp. 160-62.
6 Official Publication, 'Defence: Outline of Future Policy. 1957.', Cmnd 124, April 1957.
7 Official Publication, 'Report on Defence: Britain's Contribution to Peace and Security. 1958.', Cmnd 363, February 1958.
8 E. Spiers in D. Dilks *Retreat from Power*, Vol 2 (London: Macmillan Press, 1981) p. 160.
9 L. Freedman, op. cit., p. 16.
10 Official Publication, 'Statement on Defence, 1964', Cmnd 2270, February 1964, para 7.
11 Official Publication, 'Statement on Defence Estimates, 1965', Cmnd 2592, February 1965, para 7.
12 'Editor's Notes', *RUSI Journal*, November 1966, p. 277.
13 B. Reed and G. Williams, *Denis Healey and the Policies of Power* (London: Sidgwick and Jackson, 1971) p. 169.
14 Official Publication, 'The Future United Kingdom Strategic Nuclear Deterrent Force', DOGD 80/23. July 1980, p. 5.
15 F. Pym, 'The Nuclear Element for British Defence Policy', *RUSI Journal*, 126 June 1981, p. 4.
16 *The New Hope for Britain*, Labour's Manifesto 1983, p. 36.
17 In an interview on ITV's *Weekend World* on 28 February 1982.

5   FRENCH NUCLEAR STRATEGY

1 W. Mendl, *Deterrence and Persuasion* (London: Faber and Faber, 1970) p. 92.
2 W. L. Kohl, *French Nuclear Diplomacy* (Princeton: Princeton University Press, 1971) p. 16.
3 L. Scheinman in F. B. Horton, *Comparative Defense Policy* (Baltimore: Johns Hopkins University Press, 1974) p. 145.
4 C. de Gaulle, 'Speech at Ecole Militaire, 3 November 1959',

quoted in W. L Kohl, *French Nuclear Diplomacy*, op. cit.

5 W. L Kohl, op. cit., pp. 6-7.

6 D. S. Yost, 'French Defense Budgeting', *Orbis* 23 Fall 1979, p. 581.

7 C. de Gaulle, 'Press Conference, 23 July 1964', quoted in W. L. Kohl, *French Nuclear Diplomacy*, op. cit.

8 'Notes et etudes documentaires, No 3343', translated in *Survival*, X January 1968.

9 J. Baylis with K. Booth, J. Garnett and P. Williams, *Contemporary Strategy* (London: Croom Helm, 1975) p. 301.

10 M. Fourquet, 'The Role of Forces: Address of 3 March 1969', *Survival*, XI July 1969, p. 211.

11 Quoted in D. S. Yost, 'French Defense Budgeting', op. cit., p. 584.

12 Ibid., p. 585.

13 E. W. Basset, 'France to Modernise Nuclear Forces', *Aviation Week and Space Technology*, 16 June 1980, pp. 265-69.

14 *Strategic Survey 1980-1981* (London: International Institute for Strategic Studies, 1981) p. 80.

15 D. S. Yost, 'French Defense Budgeting', op. cit., p. 607.

16 P. Gallois, 'French Military Politics', *Bulletin of Atomic Scientists*, 37 August/September 1981, p. 23.

6 CHINESE NUCLEAR STRATEGY

1 L. Y-Y. Liu, *China as a Nuclear Power in World Politics* (London, 1972) p. 92.

2 Ibid., p. 15.

3 M. H. Halperin, *China and the Bomb* (London: Pall Mall Press, 1965) p. 80.

4 W. C. Clemens, *The Arms Race and Sino-Soviet Relations* (Stanford, 1968) p. 39

5 'Statement by Spokesman of the Chinese Government', *Peking Review*, 16 August 1963, p. 12.

6 M. Wade, 'The Chinese Ballistic Missile Program', *International Defense Review*, 8/1980, p. 1191.

7 R. Bonds (ed.), *The Chinese War Machine* (London: Salamander, 1979) p. 174.

8 *Peking Review*, 23 October 1965, p. 8.

9 *Peking Review*, 23 October 1964, p. 6.

10 *Peking Review*, 3 September 1965, pp. 26-27.

11 A. L. Hsieh, 'China's Secret Military Papers', *China Quarterly*, 18 April/June 1964, pp. 97-99.

12 Ibid., p. 86.

13 *Peking Review*, 13 May 1966, p. 4.
14 *Peking Review*, 10 October 1969, p. 20.
15 R. M Nixon, *The Real War* (London: Sidgwick and Jackson, 1980) pp. 139–40.
16 H. Gelber, 'Nuclear Weapons and Chinese Policy', *Adelphi Papers*, 99 (London: International Institute for Strategic Studies, 1973) p. 2.
17 Ibid., p. 27.
18 G. Treverton, 'China's Nuclear Forces and the Stability of Soviet-American Deterrence', *Adelphi Papers*, 160 (London: International Institute for Strategic Studies, 1980) p. 40.

7   INDIAN NUCLEAR STRATEGY

1 Quoted in B. Prasad, *India's Foreign Policy* (New Delhi: Vikas, 1979) p. 402.
2 Ibid., p. 403.
3 A. Kapur, *International Nuclear Proliferation* (New York: Praeger, 1979) p. 186.
4 A. Kapur, *India's Nuclear Option* (New York: Praeger, 1976) pp. 178–81.
5 Full text in N. Seshagiri, *The Bomb!* (New Delhi: Vikas, 1975) pp. 133–35.
6 J. P. Jain, *Nuclear India* (New Delhi: South Asia Books, 1974) p. 150.
7 Ibid., p. 91.
8 W. Epstein, 'The Proliferation of Nuclear Weapons', *Scientific American*, 232 April 1975, p. 23.
9 K. Subrahmanyam in R. M. Lawrence (ed.), *Nuclear Proliferation Phase II* (Kansas: Regents Park Press, 1974) p. 122.
10 J. P. Jain, *Nuclear India*, op. cit., p. 140.
11 A. Kapur, *International Proliferation*, op. cit., p. 173.
12 E. W. Lefever, *Nuclear Arms in the Third World* (Washington, 1979) p. 33.
13 Quoted in B. Prasad, *India's Foreign Policy*, op. cit., p. 404.
14 *New York Times*, 13 January 1978.
15 *Strategic Survey 1980-1981* (London: International Institute for Strategic Studies, 1981) p. 72.
16 E. W. Lefever, op. cit., p. 39.

8   ISRAELI NUCLEAR STRATEGY

1 F. Jabber, *Israel and Nuclear Weapons* (London: Chatto and Windus, 1971) p. 15.
2 Ibid., p. 34.

3 P. R. Chari, 'The Israeli Nuclear Option: Living Dangerously', *International Studies*, 16, September 1977, p. 347.
4 E. W. Lefever, *Nuclear Arms in the Third World* (Washington, 1979) pp. 68-69.
5 'How Israel got the Bomb', *Time*, 12 April 1976, p. 19.
6 W. Van Cleave in R. M. Lawrence (ed.), *Nuclear Proliferation Phase II* (Kansas: Regents Park Press, 1974) p. 53.
7 'CIA said in 1974 Israel had A Bombs', *New York Times*, 27 January 1978.
8 R. W. Howe, *Weapons* (London: Abacus Books, 1981) pp. 304-5.
9 T. Friedman, 'Israel's Nuclear Option', *Bulletin of Atomic Scientists*, 30, September 1974, p. 30.
10 Quoted in E. W. Lefever, *Nuclear Arms in the Third World*, op. cit., p. 67.
11 'How Israel got the Bomb', *Time*, 12 April 1976, p. 19.
12 E. W. Lefever, op. cit., p. 71.
12 S. Feldman, *Israeli Nuclear Deterrence* (New York: Columbia University Press, 1982) p. 242.

PART III

Future Stability

10   STABILITY AND AGREEMENTS

1 A. Beaufre, *Deterrence and Strategy* (London: Faber and Faber, 1965) p. 97.
2 K. N. Waltz, 'The Spread of Nuclear Weapons: More May Be Better', *Adelphi Papers* 171 (London: International Institute for Strategic Studies, 1981) p. 29.
3 C Cannizzo, 'A Critique of the Technological Approach', *Nuclear Proliferation in the 1980s*, edited by W. H. Kincade and C Bertram (London: Macmillan Press, 1982) p. 176.
4 E. P. Thompson, in *Britain and the Bomb*, New Statesman Report 3 (London, 1981) pp. 26-28.
5 MOD Public Relations Leaflet, *A Nuclear Free Europe? Why it would not work.*
6 R.L. Garwin in D.C. Gompert (ed.), *Nuclear Weapons and World Politics* (New York: McGraw Hill, 1977) pp. 104-9.
7 S. Zuckerman, *Nuclear Illusion and Reality* (London: Collins, 1982) p. 134.
8 R. L. Garthoff, 'SALT I: An Evaluation', *World Politics*, XXXI October 1978, p. 3.

9 D. O. Graham, *The Non-Nuclear Defense of Cities* (Cambridge Mass: Abt Books, 1983) pp. 1-15.

10 M. M. Lowenthal, *Nuclear Freeze Alternatives* (Washington: Library of Congress Report, 83-95f, 1983) p. 1.

11 R. L. Garthoff, op. cit., p. 10.

12 ibid., p. 12.

13 B. M. Blechman, 'Do Negotiated Arms Limitations have a Future?', *Foreign Affairs*, 59 Fall 1980, p. 115.

14 P. H. Nitze, 'Strategy in the Decade of the 1980s', *Foreign Affairs*, 59 Fall 1980, p. 94.

15 G Ignatieff in F. Griffiths (ed.), *The Dangers of Nuclear War* (Toronto: University of Toronto Press, 1979) p. 71.

16 D. Ball, 'Can Nuclear War be Controlled?', *Adelphi Papers*, 169 (London: International Institute for Strategic Studies, 1981) p. 22.

17 W. Epstein and B. T. Feld, *New Directions in Disarmament* (New York: Praeger, 1981) p. 135.

18 L. Martin, 'If you knows of a better 'ole', *The Listener*, 12 November 1981, p. 563.

19 M. Walzer, *Just and Unjust Wars* (London: Basic, 1980) pp. 282-83.

20 M. Randle, 'Defence Without the Bomb', *Proceedings of International Standing Conference on Conflict and Peace Studies* (London, 1981) p. 180.

21 D. Smith, 'Towards Alternatives: Non-Nuclear Military Options', *Proceedings of International Standing Conference on Conflict and Peace Studies* (London, 1981) p. 173.

11 STABILITY AND TECHNOLOGY

1 S. Zuckerman, *Nuclear Illusion and Reality* (London: Collins, 1982) p. 132.

2 J. S. Wit, 'Advances in Anti-submarine Warfare', *Scientific American* 244 February 1981, p. 30.

3 B. Scowcroft, *President's Commission on Strategic Forces* (Washington: The Pentagon, 1983) p. 9.

4 ESECS, *Strengthening Conventional Deterrence in Europe* (London: Macmillan Press, 1983).

5 Ibid., P. 245.

12 STABILITY AND STRATEGY

1 C. Bell, *The Diplomacy of Détente* (London: Martin Robertson, 1977) pp. 89-90.

2 P. Bracken, *The Command and Control of Nuclear Forces*

(Yale: Yale University Press, 1983) p. 2.
3 Bundy, Kennan, McNamara, Smith, 'Nuclear Weapons and the Atlantic Alliance', *Foreign Affairs*, Spring 1982.
4 M. Mandelbaum, *The Nuclear Revolution* (Cambridge: Cambridge University Press, 1981) p. 166.
5 'The Montebello Decision', *NATO Review*, No 5, 1983, p. 33.

13   CONCLUSION

1 A. Sakharov, 'The Danger of Thermonuclear War', *Foreign Affairs*, Summer 1983, p. 1016.

INDEX

INDEX